SECRETS OF A RECOVERING CONTROL FREAK

How I Finally Learned to Let God Lead Me

BETHANY COMERFORD

STOKEPUBLISHING

Contents

SECRETS OF A RECOVERING CONTROL FREAK

© 2019 Bethany Comerford
ISBN: 978-1-988675-56-5
STOKE Publishing

BONUS: Make sure you download the FREE COMPANION JOURNAL from Bethany's Website so that you can dive more deeply into the mindset work of letting God lead you.
www.positiveconnectionscoaching.com/my-book

Credits
Editing: Heather McLeskey
Author Headshot: Erica Shifflet

DISCLAIMER:
The opinions of the author are the author's alone and do not reflect the viewpoints of the Publisher.

If you feel that this book would be ideal for your coaching practice, workshops or bookclub, please contact Bethany Comerford directly for bulk purchases at:
www.positiveconnectionscoaching.com

Dedication

I would like to dedicate this book to my parents. Throughout my life they have taught me the things that truly matter in life. They taught me about Heavenly Father, and through their examples, I learned how much power and peace comes from having a testimony of Him.

I would also like to dedicate this book to my sweet husband, Cameron, and daughters, Haylee and Jori. They know the REAL me and continue to love me anyway! Their love, support, and patience helped this book become a reality.

A Note From The Author

I have created a *Companion Journal* for this book because I wanted to make it a book you can experience, not just read. I thought about the questions I would pose as a Faith-Based Life Coach if I was working privately with a client and wanted them to process the lessons on a little deeper level.

We learn lessons from stories other people share with us and we learn them on a deeper level if we are prompted with thought-provoking questions that encourage us to integrate them into our own experiences.

While this book shares my story, the *Companion Journal* **gives you the opportunity to connect my lessons to your life and challenges as well.**

The journal has ample space to reflect on the questions I pose so that you can apply the lessons I learned to your personal journey and awakening.

This journal can also be used as a discussion guide for any groups who are using this book in a coaching or study group arrangement. Please visit the link below to have the free journal sent to your email address.

www.positiveconnectionscoaching.com/my-book

Introduction

I am a control freak. I like things done a certain way (yes, there *is* a right way!). When I cannot control how something is done that I feel strongly about, it literally causes a biochemical reaction in me that makes me extremely frustrated and angry. Yeah, I've got problems! I've been this way my whole life. I was never the "go-with-the-flow" kid. My mom used to get me all prettied up to go have pictures taken, but never tell me what we were doing until we were there at the portrait studio. She knew I would fight, kick, and scream because I didn't like having my picture taken. I pouted *a lot* as a kid. One memorable experience my parents still love to talk about is when we went to a steak house for dinner and I ordered the ribs. Now, my mom made ribs often, so I knew I liked them. Well, the waiter brought the ribs I had ordered and I was shocked! These things were huge! I couldn't just pick these ribs up and eat them like I could with my mom's ribs. My initial shock turned to major disappointment and frustration so I simply refused to eat them at all. My parents told me I could use a fork to cut the meat off and eat them that way. Nope. I was done. I was upset and my mind was made up. I did not budge. I chose ("chose" being the key word here) to go hungry instead of entertaining the idea that maybe something that looks different could also be good.

I don't know about other control freaks, but I felt immense disappointment when an event in my life didn't go as I had imagined it. When I say event, this could be something as simple as the first day of school or going to the high school football game on Friday night. I am extremely visual and need to attempt to picture precisely how things will play out. There's just one problem with that process: I, unfortunately, cannot see into the future. I unknowingly set myself up for disappointment each and every time. I forgot the part about picturing other possible scenarios. I thought if I could picture how I wanted things to play out, then I could control the situation to make it come true. Wow! I sure thought highly of my abilities!

In this book, I will share some personal experiences that did not go the way I had planned. Ironically, they turned out better than I had hoped. That is not to say that each happy ending came without major trials and doubt. I struggled for years with self-doubt and the strength of my testimony as my path led me through the trial of infertility and then raising a special needs child. I learned that doing all the right things does not guarantee that you will receive everything you want. Through these experiences, I learned that my Heavenly Father knows me better than I know myself and that if I just trust Him, He will bring things into my life that I never knew I always wanted. I'll also share some priceless moments that solidify my belief that there truly are no coincidences. Everything that happens to us has a purpose and sometimes we don't understand that purpose until much later.

ONE

When the Foolproof Plan Doesn't Work

*F*or me, life is not enjoyable if I am not connecting deeply with someone. It didn't matter if it was a best friend, a boyfriend, a family member, or neighbor. I feel purposeful when I am able to really get to know someone and they feel comfortable confiding in me. I've never been one to have, or even want, a big group of friends. The quality of a friendship was definitely more important to me than the quantity of friends I had. I grew up in Flagstaff, Arizona and as soon as I could date, I had a steady boyfriend. While I do not recommend that to the youth now, it seemed to always be that way for me. I felt more like *me* when I had someone to connect with. I was lucky that I chose really good guys as boyfriends, but I could have avoided so much needless drama, heartache, and sadness had I learned to just go on dates and be okay alone. I have always been a true romantic, and basically began playing a version of "musical chairs" with boys wondering if this would be the man I would marry. I envisioned myself marrying my high school sweetheart, whoever that turned out to be! The first time I read the quote "Happiness is being married to your best friend," I decided I was going to do just that. I was going to marry my best friend. That led me to look at every friend who was a boy in a different light. I was way too young, but it didn't stop me from asking myself "Could I marry him?" While many were an obvious "no," there were some that kept me wondering for quite a while.

I will forever be grateful to my mom for talking to me often about the type of guy I should choose to marry. She helped me understand the impact that one important decision would have on the rest of my life. My mom taught me to really look at a guy's family dynamic, his parents' relationship, and specifically how that boy treats his mom. She informed me that those would be huge clues into what my future may look like with him. While she spoke of the importance of shared interests, making sure he's as social as I want to be, noticing if he does the "little things" just to make me happy, and that he treats me nicely, the main thing I remember her saying was "Find someone who makes you laugh." Humor played a big role in our home. We are a sarcastic family and quick wit goes a long way with us. From then on, I gravitated toward funny guys. Yes, I still dated guys who were a bit more on the serious side, but I kept looking for the ones who could make me laugh.

The summer after I graduated from high school I moved up to St. George, Utah to attend Dixie College (as it was named back in 1997). Staying true to my "control freak method," I had visualized how my life would play out there. My plan was to enroll in school, immediately locate my future husband, and be sealed in the Church of Jesus Christ of Latter-Day Saints temple there in St. George. I honestly saw no obstacles to this plan coming to fruition. There were so many Latter-Day Saint boys at Dixie College, it was foolproof! Because Dixie was only a two-year college at the time my plan was to obtain my associate degree there. My long-term goal was to graduate with a psychology degree from a university and become a counselor.

My plan was to enroll in school, immediately locate my future husband, and be sealed in the Church of Jesus Christ of Latter-Day Saints temple there in St. George. I honestly saw no obstacles to this plan coming to fruition. There were so many Latter-Day Saint boys at Dixie College, it was foolproof!

Along with my love of, and need, to connect with people, I really love to help them through their problems. I have been known to call myself "a fixer." If you are telling me about a problem you are struggling with in your life, my brain immediately starts trying to assess where this problem derived from, when it really started, why it is happening, and what your options are to fix it. I can't help it--it's just how my brain is wired! Becoming a counselor just seemed to be the perfect career for me. They say if you do what you love you won't have to work a day in your life!

Well, this book would be much shorter if my *foolproof* plan had worked. It did not. In fact, it not only failed, but it failed miserably. But not without teaching me some very important lessons. As far as school went, I didn't even finish my first year. I was shocked at how overwhelmed I was with all the work required for each class. It was like every single teacher I had thought that their class was the only class I was enrolled in! How was I supposed to have a social life or find the man of my dreams if I was required to be doing homework all night? Also, I was not terribly interested in any of my classes except for my public speaking class. That was the only class I excelled in (or even remember). Math and science were always hard subjects for me and what made them worse was my attitude. Why did I need these classes to be a counselor? In my mind they were a waste of time. I did not fully understand my real academic struggle until years later, but I will share that in a later chapter. But at the time, I felt very stupid, inadequate, and out of place.

Things in my dating life were definitely more exciting and fun, but did not lead to me saying "YES!" to a guy on his knee holding a beautiful ring. There was talk of marriage with one man. He was kind and thoughtful, but looking back I should have seen from the beginning that we were not right for each other. I was determined to marry my best friend and we had begun as friends so it just made sense in my mind that he was the one. My parents had met him and while they recognized that he was a great guy, they knew he was not right for me. Now that I am a parent of two daughters, I am truly amazed that they stood by quietly and supported me, only telling me their true feelings when I asked. They knew me. They knew that if they tried to tell me he wasn't "the one" for me, I would become upset and they would risk pushing me even more towards him. I can only imagine the many prayers they sent up to Heavenly Father, begging Him to intervene. Luckily, there were a few months that this man and I were apart and I had a chance to remove the rose-colored glasses and really assess our situation. It was one of the hardest things I've done, but I ended the relationship. I had come so close to my "happily ever after" that I could almost taste it, and I had decided to walk away.

After that breakup, I moved into a different apartment and made new friends. There was a big group of us consisting of my roommates and a bunch of boys we spent a lot of time with. I became good friends with one of those boys and over time started wondering if he might be who I was looking for. I was wrong. He was not interested in me that way and actually, as I learned later, was interested in my roommate. I felt used because he would often come over (no doubt, hoping she would be there) and we would hang out together. There were definitely mixed signals and I ended up very hurt and angry at him. I was talking to my mom on the phone about the situation (she has always been my sounding board) and telling her my plan to let this guy have it! I was going to tell him how he'd hurt me and what a big jerk he was! I felt completely justified, so much so, that it caught me off guard when my mom stopped me and said "You just need to be nice to him."

My wise mother took that opportunity to teach me a couple of life lessons that I have never forgotten. The first lesson was that while I may be justified in my anger, being nasty to him wouldn't change the situation and would only make *me* look bad. She taught me that I would never regret being kind. That lesson led to another lesson, which is that people tend to come back in your life somehow. Whether it's the person themselves or a friend or relative of theirs, you would hate to feel a moment of regret for how you acted or how you treated someone. I knew she was right, and as tough as it was for me, from that day on, I plastered a smile on my face whenever I was around that boy. Over time, the tension and awkwardness between us began to fade. Just to prove that my mom's advice was correct, a few months after moving away from

St. George I came back for a visit. Ironically, this same guy (who I had no interest in anymore) was intent on spending time with me. He even expressed his desire for me to move back. I have to believe that had I gone with my original plan to make him miserable just as he had made me, he would not be interested in having me around! And I would be lying if I didn't admit that it felt really good to be the one to tell *him* that I was no longer interested (in the kindest way possible, of course).

Our ultimate goal here on earth is to become like our Savior, Jesus Christ. It can be incredibly difficult to react as He might have when people hurt us or make us angry, especially when the hurt is intentional. Through this experience, I learned that my behavior and reaction to being hurt and angry, whether good or bad, demonstrates my willingness to truly live as the Savior lived. It has nothing to do with the person who upsets me. We each face opportunities daily to be an example of the Savior. Some opportunities are small, such as an encounter with a stranger at the grocery store. Others are much more strenuous and demand that we let go of our natural human desire to retaliate. This is not an easy task, but I have learned that as we practice being kind instead of angry, it becomes easier over time.

TWO

Learning to Let Go of the Branch

*a*fter just one year in St. George, I was now back to square one with my plan. Only now I had no interest in college. A part of me felt like a failure and that maybe my decision to move to St. George had been a mistake. I am, once again, so grateful to my mom who taught me that there are no mistakes, only learning experiences. If I learned from my experience then it served its purpose. I decided to move back to Flagstaff and into an apartment with some friends from church and get a job and work full time. I did take a couple of courses at the community college there, but wasn't really focused on working toward my degree. After about a year, I felt that being in Flagstaff was not where I wanted to be. I had made some good friends and had a lot of fun, but I wanted to experience something new. One Sunday evening while at my parents' house for dinner, I was telling them how I wanted to move again. They asked where I would go and I said maybe down to Mesa (a couple of hours away). I had moved to St. George alone, and this time I wanted someone to move with me. Unfortunately, none of my good friends were in a position to move from Flagstaff at the time. I left my parents' house frustrated that this new plan just wasn't meant to be.

Now, if you talk to me today, it won't be long until you hear me say that I do not believe in coincidences. I believe everything is meant to happen the way it does. When I returned to my apartment that same evening, I received a phone call from an old friend who was living in Prescott, Arizona at the time. We had been close friends in junior high before her family moved from Flagstaff to Prescott. Our birthdays are ten days apart in April and we rarely talked except for a phone call to say "happy birthday" to each other once a year. This evening was not in April, so I was a little caught off guard by her call. As long as I live, I will never forget what she said after we got through the small talk. She said, "I know this is kind of crazy and it probably won't even work, but I want to move down to Mesa. I don't want to move alone and I wondered if maybe you might want to move with me and we could get an apartment together?" I almost fell over in shock! Did she really just say what I think she said? I probably caught her off guard when, without any hesitation, I shouted "Yes!"

As I think back to that evening, I am unable to deny the hand of Heavenly Father in that experience. I know He wanted me to continue to grow and progress, and He agreed that I needed a new environment in order to do that. I understand that He cannot always bless us with everything we wish for in the moment, but when the opportunity permits, I know He can, and is overjoyed to, perform miracles in our lives if that is what we need. Heavenly Father was able to bless my friend and I with what we both desperately desired by bringing us back together. A few years down the road, I was able to see another reason I believe He brought us back into each other's lives as this dear friend lost her husband of only about eight months. I was able to go support her through the funeral preparations and the funeral itself. I will never forget the quiet moments we spent talking and crying at night in the apartment she had shared with her sweet husband. It's interesting that as life often does, it has, once again, pulled this sweet friend and I away from each other geographically, but I am sure that we would both drop everything at a moment's notice to help the other. There are just some friends that you have that deep bond with where the friendship doesn't require daily (or even monthly) communication. I am so grateful Heavenly Father put her in my life.

The coincidences didn't end there. Around that same time, I had been introduced to a couple guys, Jeff and Cameron, from Show Low, Arizona through my best friend, Kym. She had moved to Flagstaff from Show Low her freshman year of high school (my sophomore year) and we instantly clicked and became best friends. I knew Jeff and Cameron were also moving down to Mesa, but had no idea, until we all moved down, that we were living in apartments just a block away from each other! It was so nice to have some more friends in this new big city we were adjusting to. They had just graduated from high school and were preparing to leave on missions the following year. Cameron and I became really good friends while living in Mesa. He had a girlfriend in another town and I had begun dating a guy I had dated in high school, who also lived in another town. There was no thought of us dating each other since we were both already "taken" and he was preparing to leave for two years, so we were able to be open and honest when we were together without fear of rejection. I'll never forget one afternoon while hanging out in my apartment, Cameron jokingly said, "I'm going to take you out on a date tonight!" We went to a Mexican restaurant called Macayos and had the best time together. Cameron always struck me as a funny guy, and I remember writing in my journal that night: "Went on a date with Cameron. He is hilarious! It became apparent to me how important it will be to marry someone who makes me laugh."

One minor detail I had not paid much attention to up until this point was a somewhat hidden (or buried) desire I had to serve a mission. My patriarchal blessing talks specifically about going on a mission "if I chose to." This should have been a clue that I probably would not be married before I turned 21, but I didn't pay attention to it because I had my own plan, remember? At this point in my life I was 20 years old and starting to really contemplate the idea of a mission. In fact, I was getting really excited about the idea. I remember at Christmas time being at my parents' house with my grandparents and just blurting out at the dinner table, "I'm going to go on a mission!" I had made the final decision. I still had about four months before I turned 21, but I was anxious to get the paperwork started. I remember there was a section in the paperwork for "special requests" for where you were assigned to serve. My inner control freak came out and I made three requests: third world country, Spanish speaking, and humidity. If I was going to serve a mission, I wanted it to be a truly different experience. I had taken Spanish in school and while I was nowhere near fluent, I knew the rules of grammar and felt prepared to learn to speak that language fluently. As for the humidity, I have naturally curly hair, although I rarely wear it that way. I knew I would not have much time each day to get ready and that would be the most time efficient way to do it. If it was humid, it would curl better, and therefore, look better. Yes, my hair is *that* important to me (I am a hairdresser's daughter)! When I had my final interview with my stake president before sending in my papers, he noticed that section, smiled to himself and asked me, "So what will you do if you get called to Temple Square in Salt Lake?" I confidently replied that I would happily accept whatever call I received. But secretly, I was really hoping my requests would be granted!

While I was still living in Mesa, my mission call arrived at my parents' house in Flagstaff. Cameron had been called to the Ohio Cleveland Mission and his farewell was the following weekend. My boyfriend and I drove to his farewell in Show Low, then went on to Flagstaff to open my mission call. I was called to the Dominican Republic Santo Domingo West Mission and I was called to teach the gospel in Spanish! I was excited I had at least gotten my wish to speak Spanish! But I had never heard of the Dominican Republic! We pulled a map out and the first thing I noticed was Haiti and I got worried! The Dominican Republic and Haiti share the same island in the Caribbean. I had heard of Haiti, but everything I'd heard wasn't good. Nevertheless, I was excited. All three of my special requests had been granted! I believe some part of me was drawn to where I would end up serving, without even knowing it existed! I was so excited to begin learning all I could about the country I would spend the next 18 months in.

As I mentioned before, I was also dating someone I had dated previously and, given our history, I think we both believed we were meant to be together. After I received my mission call, he said he would wait for me and we would get married when I returned. But a few weeks before my farewell he admitted to me that he couldn't promise that he would be able to wait for me. I was blindsided by this and started to question whether I should leave or not.

I recalled another lesson my mom had taught me about life being like a river. I am sure it was yet another attempt to help me learn to not be such a control freak. She explained to me that when I tried to make things happen (or control things) that weren't happening naturally it was like while flowing down a river, I had grabbed onto a branch and wouldn't let go. She said it seemed like I had been flowing great, but now a branch had presented itself and I was hanging on for dear life. She encouraged me to pray to find out what I should do. I think I already knew what the answer would be, but I knelt down and prayed as she had suggested, which led to an experience I will never forget--an experience I shared at my farewell.

After I finished telling Heavenly Father all about my dilemma and how I felt, I asked for His guidance. I needed to be confident in whichever choice I made. Then I stayed on my knees for a few minutes and a scene presented itself in my mind. It was of me sitting with a woman in a dark room of a house. The only light was from a few candles on a table. I looked down and saw my missionary name tag on the dress I was wearing. The woman I was sitting with was crying and the room was very somber. She had lost a child to death and I heard myself promising her that she would, in fact, see that child again. I could feel her clinging to the words I was saying, hope filling her broken heart. I had my answer. I felt it. I needed to go serve my mission. I had no idea if this would prove to happen in the way I had pictured it, but I felt the urgent need to share the truth of the gospel I knew and loved with those who didn't have it. I had to go.

THREE

This is What I Wanted—But Why is it So Hard?

I arrived at the Missionary Training Center (MTC) in Provo, Utah on May 3, 2000. I was so excited to be there! I met my companion and we instantly hit it off. Things were great! Little did I know, I was about to have yet another experience that would prove to me that coincidences do not exist and that Heavenly Father cares about even the tiniest desires of our hearts.

Ever since my family had visited the Polynesian Cultural Center on the island of Oahu in Hawaii when I was a teenager, I had wanted to serve a mission in the Polynesian islands, specifically Tonga or Samoa. I had heard a rumor, though, that sister missionaries were not sent there because the of the risk of danger, so I gave up on that wish long before putting in my papers to serve. Our first afternoon in the MTC, my companion and I went to the assigned room where we would meet the other members of our district. We would spend all day and evening with these people for the next eight weeks. As we sat there, in walked three Tongan elders (two from Tonga, the other from California) and one Samoan sister! I was beside myself with shock and excitement! Since I couldn't serve my mission on those islands, Heavenly Father had brought those people to me! I spent my time in the MTC surrounded by their culture--the beautiful music, the laughter and light-heartedness, and even the food! One of the counselors in our Branch Presidency happened to return from a trip to Hawaii and surprised our district one evening with kalua pig meat! It was amazing! I formed such strong bonds with these other missionaries. They became like family for those two months in the MTC.

Everyone in our district left the MTC the same morning, with the exception of the Tongan elder from California and myself. After spending every day and evening together for eight long weeks, to say we were sad would be a huge understatement. We were heart-broken and the tears were unstoppable. I had learned first-hand how intense a bond can be when you struggle together and also have numerous spiritual experiences together as a group. It felt so unnatural that we should be separated now and I felt like a part of me was now gone. What was even harder to accept, was the thought that I may never see these people every again. My last day at the MTC was extremely depressing. I was ready to leave. It felt wrong and uncomfortable to be there without them.

Ironically, I flew out of the United States to the Dominican Republic on July 4, 2000. That was by far, the oddest 4th of July I have ever experienced! I traveled with a group of elders and upon arrival in our mission, we were taken to the tourist spots in the capital to explore a little bit. Later that evening, I was taken to the "Hermana Mansion" ("hermana" means "sister" in Spanish) in Santo Domingo where the sisters lived in that area. This house was where all the new sisters spent their first night and all the sisters going home spent their last night in the mission. The sisters serving in that area took me along with them to their appointments that evening and it all became very real for me. All of my senses were overloaded! Although I was very aware of the poverty level in the Dominican Republic, it was quite a shock to experience it in person. To see homes and tiny shacks that I had only seen in photographs of other third world countries or on television was a bit jarring. There was noise everywhere! Motorcycles buzzing down the street past us, loud music coming from every direction, men hissing like snakes at women (including us), people talking on the street--it felt chaotic to me! There were so many different smells attacking me at once--fried meat being sold on the street, old, wet trash in alley ways that we tried our best to step over, strong perfume and cologne on the younger people who were out to have a good time. And then there was the touching!

I have another confession: I am not a touchy person by nature. I welcome hugs, but I am not quick to offer them. This has absolutely nothing to do with how I feel about a person. I just tend to keep my hands to myself really well! It couldn't be more opposite for Dominicans! They are extremely affectionate and warm people. The standard greeting is two kisses, one on each cheek. I was already being thrust out of my comfort zone the first night!

Among all of these different observations and the sensory overload I was experiencing, was a much more powerful feeling. The love between these sisters I was with and the Dominican people they were visiting was almost palpable. They didn't bat an eye at the smells, sounds, or sights that were almost overpowering me. It was like they didn't even notice any of the chaos was there. I watched as they sat and had meaningful, joyful, and spiritual conversations (none of which I could understand) with these people. I prayed at that moment that I would be able to get to their level quickly, not just with the language, but more importantly, with their ability to adapt to this new lifestyle.

The first area I was assigned was a little town called Nizao. I got along with my companion right away, a sister from Utah, which was such a blessing. She was very understanding as I was trying to adjust to what would be my new life during my mission in this country. Our house was one of the nicer homes in the town and we slept in mosquito nets that hung from the ceiling above our beds and took bucket baths (where you stand in the bathtub and pour cold water over yourself with a bucket). I was getting the full experience I had hoped for right off the bat! It wasn't long before I was able to experience an almost daily phenomenon which would test my desire to control things. In the Dominican Republic, the electricity randomly and frequently goes out. When this happens, you'll hear people say, "Se fue la luz," being translated loosely, "The light went out." There is absolutely no warning when this will happen. I remember one particularly miserable night experiencing this. As I mentioned before, we slept in mosquito nets that surrounded our beds and we each had our own electric fan to keep us cool throughout the night. One night the electricity went out around 2a.m. and it turned incredibly hot and humid almost instantly. I was miserable. I knew I wouldn't be able to go back to sleep until the electricity came back on, but not knowing when that might be, I got up, grabbed a wooden chair from the table, went out to the front porch, propped my chair up against the house, and sat there just praying for a breeze!

I believe that we are put in positions and places, far from our comfort zone, to help us grow. The hope is that we will acknowledge our weaknesses and begin working on making them strengths. I am very aware now of how my need to control things is not a strength and is something I need to work on. But while I was on my mission, I believed the ability to take control *was* a strength. I naively believed that being able to control situations was a sign of maturity, independence, and competency. Unfortunately, I had been placed in a country, mission, and multiple individual situations that I could not, and honestly, should not have been able to control. The greatest and most frustrating issue that challenged my need for control on my mission was punctuality.

I believe that we are put in positions and places, far from our comfort zone, to help us grow. The hope is that we will acknowledge our weaknesses and begin working on making them strengths. I am very aware now of how my need to control things is not a strength and is something I need to work on. But while I was on my mission, I believed the ability to take control was a strength.

I do not like showing up late to anything. When I was younger, this stemmed from a fear of drawing unwanted attention to myself. I did not want everyone in the room to turn and look at me as I entered. As I got older, I saw a late arrival as a form of disrespect (have I mentioned that I am a huge rule follower?). I believe it showed a lot about a person's willingness, or lack thereof, to manage their time so that they can not only be on time, but preferably early to an event. After many weeks of frustration in Nizao, this issue came to a head between my companion and I. We had a "charla" (discussion) scheduled for 2 p.m. and it was 1:55 p.m. We still had a nearly 20-minute walk to the house where we would have our discussion. I was incredibly frustrated (there may very well have been smoke coming out of my ears!) and worried about how our investigator would feel when we arrived so late. Would she be angry? Would she still be there waiting for us at all? I angrily expressed my thoughts to my ever-patient companion and her response took me by surprise. She smiled, almost chuckled, and said, "Hermana ("sister"), you need to take your watch off." I stared blankly back at her, so she continued, "Dominicans, as a whole, don't usually care about time like we do. There is a good chance we will show up 20 minutes late to this charla and she won't even be ready for us!" And guess what? My companion was right! As the door to the home opened, our investigator greeted us and said, "You're early!" We assured her we were not early, and I apologized for actually being quite late. She was not bothered in the least.

Dominicans handled time differently and I needed to adapt. I needed to loosen up and learn to "flow" with their culture. I realize now that one reason I needed to serve in that type of culture was so that I could learn that lesson. I needed to be immersed in a culture that I had no power to change. It was important for me to see that although these characteristics I had were viewed as strengths back home, they were obnoxious and unattractive here in this culture. Showing up on time was not the priority here. Loving people, being patient, and trying to be understanding were their priorities. Allowing myself to adjust to their way of life would serve me better than trying to get them to adapt to my ways. Once I was able to accept this new way of thinking, I was happier, calmer, and able to focus so much more on the people individually. My relationships with them became more meaningful, and I was becoming the person I needed to be for what lay ahead in my mission.

FOUR

Once You've Pulled Yourself Out of the Ditch, Reach Back for Others

---

*R*eturned missionaries often say that their mission was the best two years (or 18 months for sisters) of their life. I have heard this corrected to "the best two years/18 months *for* their life". I am so grateful for that little correction because my mission was hard! As I mentioned before, I had taken Spanish in school and was fairly competent, at least with basic phrases and verb conjugations. That might have served me well in another Spanish speaking mission, but Dominican Spanish is extremely different. Their own personal accent makes understanding them very difficult. They often remove the letter "s" from their words, they tend to leave off the ends of words, and some of them just talk really fast! It took me a few months to really be able to understand the people when they spoke to me.

As October General Conference approached, just three months since I'd arrived in the mission, my excitement grew. I wasn't just excited, I was desperate. The "greenie excitement" ("greenie" is a nickname for a new missionary) had worn off and it had sunk in that I would be here for a little over another year. I needed the strong spirit that the talks from President Hinckley and the other general authorities would surely bring, and my companion had assured me that we would be able to listen to conference in English at the church. The week leading up to General Conference was an especially hard one. The work was slow, and we had shown up to many charlas to find nobody home. As a missionary, when the work is slow it makes every other hard thing feel ten times worse. I was feeling somewhat defeated, but I knew I would be able to find the spiritual sustenance to relight the fire of my testimony as a missionary during General Conference.

The first day of General Conference came and as we arrived at the chapel, we were quickly informed that they were not able to hook up the English translation. There was nothing anyone could do to fix it. Once again, I was placed in a situation I had zero control over. Unfortunately, that was the straw that broke this camel's back! Hot tears sprung to my eyes and I felt a despair I had never felt before. Didn't Heavenly Father understand how badly I needed to hear these messages in my own language? Yes, by this point I could understand Spanish for the most part, but I *needed* to hear it in my native language. I didn't feel I had the energy necessary to put forth the extra work to translate the words in my brain. I just wanted the words and spirit to flow in. I felt I deserved that blessing and, quite frankly, I felt I had earned it after all I had been through that week.

After the morning session we walked over to the Zone Leaders' house for lunch. I was emotionally exhausted and ended up out on the balcony asleep on a mattress. I had made a good friend in that zone named Elder Ross. He was nearing the end of his mission as I was just beginning. We normally gave each other a hard time and joked around a lot. He could tell I was upset and while I was asleep, he had asked my companion what was wrong with me. She explained the week we had been through and my frustration at not being able to hear General Conference in English. They reminisced about when they had first arrived in the mission and how hard the adjustment could be.

The next morning when we showed up for the Sunday morning session of General Conference (still in Spanish), Elder Ross handed me a plate of homemade brownies. He explained that he felt I probably needed a little something that would remind me of home. In that moment I learned that even when things don't go the way we would like, for reasons we may never understand, Heavenly Father will bless us with people to help "soften the blow" and give us the strength we need to keep going. Elder Ross told me that he understood how I was feeling because he had been in my position at one point, too. But then he spoke from experience and assured me that it would get better. He was honest and said it would still be hard sometimes, but that I would be able to get through those hard times and that it would be worth all the frustration.

While I was grateful for those amazing brownies (as I believe chocolate can fix almost anything), I was even more grateful and touched that Elder Ross had noticed my frustration and reached out to help. I don't believe that we are meant to just *survive* our trials. I believe that after we have overcome a trial and have learned the lesson, we should then turn around and reach out to those who are still struggling to make it through. We now have a special ability to connect with them and be an instrument in Heavenly Father's hands to bless them. One of my favorite quotes is by President Spencer W. Kimball. It states, "God does notice us and he watches over us, but it is usually through another person that He meets our needs" ("Small Acts of Service." *Ensign*, December

1974). I do not believe there is a more rewarding feeling than when we realize our actions were a direct answer to another person's prayer. When we realize that Heavenly Father was able to count on us to help one of His children, we can't help but feel honored, as well as just a bit nearer to Him.

FIVE

The Rest of the Story

*E*lder Ross was right, things did get better. In fact, the following transfer I was sent to a little town called Cambita, and was made senior companion. They were taking out the elders that were serving in that area and replacing them with sisters.

My companion would actually be a sister who I had first met in the MTC. One day at lunch in the cafeteria, we had passed each other and noticed we had on the same exact dress, just in different colors! We asked the other where they were called to serve their mission and were shocked to discover we'd be going to the same mission! We joked about how funny it would be if we were able to serve as companions and wear our matching dresses! The second time I saw her, shortly after I arrived in the mission, my first companion and I had the opportunity to go work at the open house for the Santo Domingo Dominican Republic temple. This meant leaving our area to go to the capital where we would stay overnight at the home of the sister missionaries serving in the nearest area. Come to find out, that same sister missionary from the MTC was one of those sisters in that house! We had such a great time together and now talked about our hope that we would be made companions at some point. The very next transfer our hope was realized! We couldn't believe our luck!

As companions, there is very little time apart from each other. Being placed with a companion you enjoy being around is one of the biggest tender mercies during a mission. This companion and I had such a great time together, but we also worked very hard. We felt useful in Cambita with the members there and we were having some great spiritual experiences together. It was one of the happiest times on my mission. After one special experience I had in Cambita, I knew I would never forget that place and it would forever have a special place in my heart.

We had been teaching a woman there for a couple weeks and we had bonded pretty quickly. She was married, had one daughter, and was pregnant with her second child. This woman was very intelligent and had a pretty comfortable lifestyle. She loved to have us over and cook for us. We were very surprised and disappointed one day when we showed up at her house for our scheduled appointment and were told by a relative that she wasn't able to meet with us. The relative mentioned something about her being sick, but it just felt odd the way he was explaining it. At the time, there were still many Spanish words, phrases, and terms I was not familiar with and I just assumed I was not understanding him very well. We asked him to tell her we loved her and headed back out to the street. Being stood up as missionaries is not uncommon, but there are some people you meet that you don't expect that from. She was one of those people. We were so confused.

This incident weighed heavy on my companion and I for a couple of days. One night as we were out walking, the electricity went out. This makes it even tougher to meet people as you can hardly see anything. We were near the home of that same woman and I suggested we stop by just to see if she was feeling better. To our surprise, she answered the door herself and invited us in. We sat in her dark living room, lit only by a few candles, and made small talk. She said she had, in fact, been sick, but was better now. There was something different about her though. She seemed closed off to us. She seemed stiff. Our awkward conversation felt like that of a new acquaintance. But this was a good friend of ours. Something wasn't right. I couldn't stand it any longer and I looked at her and quietly asked, "What is going on with you? Something is wrong and I can feel it. Please be honest with us." She said nothing for a moment, then I saw her eyes fill with tears. When she was able to speak, she said, "I lost the baby." In an instant, my mind raced back in time to that scene I had had in my mind after praying about my decision to serve a mission or stay home. Was this really happening? I looked around. Here I was in a dark room, lit only by candles on a table. I looked back at her and with a shaky voice and tears in my eyes, I said, "You are why I am here on my mission. You will see your child again." I don't know that I've ever felt the Spirit as strong I did that night in her home. We were part of each other's plan here on earth. I had been sent all the way from Arizona to the Dominican Republic to assure her that she had not lost that child forever.

I would love to be able to say that after that experience she chose to be baptized, but that was not the case. Although we had shared a very special experience together, she had other reasons for not feeling ready to accept our invitation to be baptized at that time. While missionaries serve with the intention and purpose of helping people accept baptism, we are also taught that every time we share the gospel with someone, we are planting a seed. Our success was not to be measured by the number of people we taught and baptized, but on the moments we were able to share our testimony of the gospel and help others feel the Holy Ghost in their lives. I know our friend felt the Holy Ghost that night in her home. I know that her despair was replaced by hope. Whether that experience would lead to her choosing to be baptized or not, Heavenly Father saw her need to be comforted. She was His child and he loved her. I will forever be grateful that my companion and I were able to provide that assurance.

She said nothing for a moment, then I saw her eyes fill with tears. When she was able to speak, she said, "I lost the baby." In an instant, my mind raced back in time to that scene I had had in my mind after praying about my decision to serve a mission or stay home. Was this really happening?

SIX

Tragic Events Can Reveal True Feelings

*R*eceiving mail as a missionary is crucial to your happiness! In my mission, we only got mail once a week on P-day (Preparation day-a sort of day off from missionary work). Therefore, P-day was either really good or really disappointing, depending on how many letters we received. Receiving packages was even better! My friend Cameron was serving in the Ohio Cleveland Mission. He had left for the MTC three months before I did and a couple weeks after getting there he wrote me a letter telling me how frustrated he was that he was not hearing from as many people from home as he expected, people who had promised to send letters. I made a deal with him back then that if he would write me a letter every week, I would do the same for him, thus guaranteeing us at least one letter each week. Cameron went above and beyond our deal and when I arrived at the MTC I already had a package waiting for me from him!

Writing to Cameron was a huge blessing and help to me during my mission. Although our living and mission circumstances were almost completely opposite from one another, he was also far from home trying to share the gospel. In my mission, we were encouraged to try to keep our letters to our parents as positive as we could. There was no email back then and letters often took about three weeks to be delivered. If we wrote all about how much we were struggling, our parents wouldn't even know about it until weeks later, when the issue was most likely resolved. My parents have since explained to me just how helpless parents feel when they read in a letter that their child is struggling. While they are fully aware that the mission will be challenging, keeping the negative things on a "need to know" basis makes it more bearable. With Cameron, I had someone I could write to about those challenges and tough times. Even better, he could relate to me, validate my feelings, and encourage me.

We tried to send each other pictures as much as possible. We also recorded ourselves talking on cassette tapes and sent those. Tapes were the best! It was so fun and reassuring to hear each other's voices. I remember about halfway through my mission I received a package from Cameron. It had tapes and pictures inside, so I was thrilled! We usually opened mail with all the other missionaries in the zone and there was a rule that if you received pictures you had to pass them around for everyone to see (we were all so desperate for anything new!). I remember a specific picture of Cameron at the Cleveland Cavaliers basketball game (in his mission they were allowed to attend two sporting events a year--I was extremely jealous!). As my companion at that time looked at the photo, she remarked, "He's handsome!" I snatched the picture back and looked at it. Wait, how had I not noticed that before? He *was* handsome! From that moment on, something changed in the way I felt about Cameron. I had never looked at him that way before. I didn't ever say anything to him about how my feelings had started to change because we were still missionaries, after all. There were some things he said in letters and on tapes that gave me the idea that he might be looking at me differently as well, but we never discussed that topic. Everything remained pretty much the same between us. That is, until September 11, 2001.

The morning of September 11, 2001 began just as every other day had for my companion and I. I was serving in Quisqueya, and only had about two months left of my mission. I had a great companion, another sister from Utah, and we had been able to convince our mission president to keep us together through a few transfers because we were working hard and got along great.

As we were walking through narrow walkways between homes, an old lady who was sweeping her porch stopped us and asked, "Are you Americans?" We told her that we were and she replied, "Your buildings are falling." This made absolutely no sense to us. As missionaries, we had no access to television or radio, so we were oblivious to any news. In all honesty, we just assumed she was a little senile, so we smiled politely and continued on our way.

We hadn't walked but a few steps when we passed an open doorway. There was a television turned on just inside the home and although there were about five or six people surrounding it, I was able to see they were watching the news. As they noticed that the only two American women in town had stopped and were peeking in, their eyes grew large and they invited us in quickly to sit down. We soon realized what we were seeing, but couldn't quite register why it was happening. Listening to the news in Spanish made it even more difficult to process. After watching for about fifteen or twenty minutes we decided we should go back to our house where we could be contacted by the mission office with any special instructions. Shortly after we were told to resume normal activities, our next-door neighbors knocked on our door. They were a sweet older couple from Puerto Rico and they knew we didn't have a television. They were worried we hadn't heard the news. We told them what we had seen and they said, "We have television in English if you'd like to watch it so you can understand better." I was so grateful for their thoughtfulness. We went over to their home and while sitting in wooden rocking chairs, we watched the events that were changing our home country.

I don't know that I will ever be able to describe how odd and detached I felt that day. It was a strange feeling to see such tragedy happening in my country, but for the most part, life around me continued on as usual. Although it seems almost every Dominican knows someone or has family that either lives or works in New York, and they were all trying to find out if they were okay, this country I was in was not under attack like my country back home was. That day was the last time I saw any news about September 11, 2001 until the following year. Nobody talked too much about it with us after they learned we were not from New York. Life marched on for us as it had the day before.

A few weeks later, I got the first letter from Cameron after September 11th. Even on paper, I could tell he was not his normal, funny self. He told me how different things were now back home. In all the uneasiness and confusion, he said there were rumors among the missionaries of a military draft that he feared being pulled into. I could feel his fear and I realized all I had been oblivious to, living so far away. We had always ended our letters by saying "I love you". Up until now it was always meant in a friendly, platonic, caring way. This letter was different. Cameron ended it by saying, "I wish I could call you. All I want to do is talk to you. I love you, Bethany." It is amazing how those three words can take on a whole new meaning just by adding a person's name! It was that moment that I knew he felt the same about me as I had grown to feel about him.

SEVEN

Heavenly Father Can ALWAYS Make Your Plan Better

*A*nother lesson I have been grateful to have been taught is that you can receive spiritual promptings and answers to personal questions in a class, meeting, or any setting where the Spirit is present, regardless of the topic being discussed. For example, you may be listening to a talk about tithing and feel a strong prompting to read your scriptures more. As long as the Spirit is felt, it can touch each person individually regarding their own lives.

I would be lying if I said my companion and I didn't talk often about Cameron after I received that letter. I was just about finished with my mission and "real life" would begin for me very soon. Cameron wouldn't return home from his mission until three months after I did. Was he "the one?" Was I supposed to wait for him after I got home? Being the true control freak that I am, I wanted the answers to these questions now!

One day, my companion and I were sitting on the front porch of an old man's home sharing favorite scriptures with him. He was so kind and it was such a neat experience taking turns explaining what different scriptures meant to us and the peace they brought to us. At one point, while he was reading a scripture out loud, my mind wandered a bit to my situation with Cameron. I immediately got this warm feeling of peace and I knew, as sure as the sky was blue, that he was the one I was supposed to marry. As we left that man's porch and headed home, I told my companion of the experience I had just had. She didn't even question it. When the Spirit speaks, you don't argue! Some might find it odd that I would receive that clear answer while still serving my mission. Even I was surprised! I would later learn why Heavenly Father had blessed me with that little tender mercy.

I returned home from my mission in November of 2001. It was quite an adjustment from tropical, humid weather to cold, painful winter weather in Flagstaff! I couldn't handle it so I moved back down to Mesa pretty quickly. I'll admit, one of the very best things about being back in the United States (and there were many things!) was being able to send letters and packages to Cameron and know that he would get them in just a few days, not three weeks! I already felt so much closer to him. We still did not discuss our relationship while he was finishing his mission, but it was obvious we felt the same about one another. We wrote a lot about fun things we would go do after he returned. We had become so much closer through two years of weekly letters. We'd had the benefit of being able to ask each other questions about likes and dislikes, dreams and goals for the future, and more. Those last three months of his mission seemed to drag on forever! Finally, though, the day came. I would go to the airport with my friends to see him arrive. But amid the excitement I was feeling, the first of two doubts started to creep into my mind.

I am a strong believer in "the spark." The spark is that immediate physical attraction to someone. I'd had enough experiences with great guys who would have made wonderful husbands, but the spark just wasn't there. And you can't create the spark. It's either there or it's not. Believe me, I had tried incredibly hard with all of my controlling power to force it a couple of times, but to no avail. What if the spark wasn't there when I saw him? I had never looked at Cameron that way before. What a cruel trick it would be to have gotten so close to him, to the point of picturing the rest of my life with him, only to find that I would always see Cameron as just a good friend! But then I thought back to that day on my mission. That day I knew, with total certainty, that I was supposed to marry Cameron. I was given that answer. I tried to focus on that certainty as I stood with our friends and waited to see Cameron come walking out of the terminal at the airport.

And then there he was! I knew the second I saw him. There wasn't just a spark, there were fireworks! I could finally relax and enjoy the moment. Our friends and I were all standing in the back of the crowd, letting Cameron's family welcome him home first. While that makes me sound generous, I was in the back in an attempt to keep the embarrassment factor to a minimum. Although Cameron and I hadn't discussed our relationship with each other, we had obviously made it pretty clear to others how we felt about one another. I knew that all eyes would be on the two of us when it was my turn to talk to him.

It was such a strange, but exciting feeling as Cameron approached me. Here was the guy who had not only become my best friend, but also the man I was in love with. Hugging him was almost magical. Over the past two years he had become so important to me, like my missing piece. I felt whole again. That day in the airport is one of my top five favorite memories with Cameron. It's one of my very favorite daydreams.

I often think back to when I was a teenager thinking about who I might marry. I had said I wanted to marry someone who would make me laugh. I had said I would marry my best friend. In all my searching for that special guy, I had never considered Cameron, even while he was right in front of me! I couldn't see it at the time, but I can now see all the little steps Heavenly Father took to bring us together. Once again, there are no coincidences. I believe every situation plays out the way it is supposed to as long as we are trying to keep Heavenly Father in our lives. If we turn our will over to Him, He will take what we want (or what we think we want) and make it so much better! Every single time!

EIGHT

True Joy Cannot Be Hidden

*T*he funniest part about the day Cameron returned home, was after we left the airport. Cameron drove with his parents over to the apartment complex I lived in with my friends and while still wearing his suit and missionary name tag, he signed the lease for the apartment just above ours along with our good friend Brett. This was something we had discussed prior to him coming home. It sure was a good thing that spark was there!

It was Friday afternoon and we all headed up to Show Low where Cameron's parents lived. Cameron rode with his family while my friend, Kym, and I drove up in my car. Kym's parents also lived in Show Low, so we would stay at their home. That evening, after Cameron had been released as a missionary, Kym and I drove over to his house where we sat and visited with him and his family in their living room.

I will never forget how comfortable and wonderful it felt to sit next to Cameron on that couch, talking for hours about anything that came to mind. It was so nice to see his facial expressions and get immediate answers to questions, rather than waiting for those answers in a letter. Even in that moment, I remember thinking to myself, "How did you not ever realize that he was exactly what you were looking for all along?" Whatever the answer to that question was, I realized it now. I had never been happier or more excited about the future. I had no idea another doubt would be taking control of my mind and emotions soon.

The next evening, a bunch of our friends gathered at Cameron's home to visit and watch movies. I am somewhat embarrassed to admit I was having a tough time sharing him! Anyone who knows Cameron understands what a social butterfly he is. He is a big hugger and he has the ability to make you feel like the most important and amazing person. He is always happy and upbeat and loves to have fun. I knew I better get used to sharing him. And honestly, the tradeoff was always in my favor. He was worth it.

It was late when the movie ended and everyone had gone home except for Kym and I. She had fallen asleep in the recliner across the room. Cameron and I sat there talking a little longer, not wanting the night to end. Eventually, we realized how tired we were, so we stood up and Cameron naturally insisted on a hug (as if I would argue!) before I left. As I pulled away after a ridiculously long squeeze, he leaned down and kissed me. Well, if I thought there were fireworks that day at the airport, then this was a full-fledged 4th of July extravaganza! It was perfect. He was perfect. Everything was perfect!

The Snowflake Temple dedication was the following morning. My parents were coming from Flagstaff for the dedication and Cameron's parents had invited them to come over later that afternoon to visit. It was the perfect, low-pressure setting for our families to get to know each other, or more realistically, for everyone to have a chance to scope the other family out! My mom had met Cameron a couple times before our missions. I remember her saying back then how mature he seemed. But my dad had yet to meet the man who his youngest daughter was in love with. I was not concerned. To know Cameron (even if you aren't me) is to love him.

I don't believe those few hours together could have been any more perfect. Cameron's mom, his sister, and Cameron himself all play the guitar. Why is this significant? My dad is an incredibly talented guitarist. We didn't just sit and talk in that living room; we jammed! It was a scene I never would have pictured myself in! And yet, it was amazing! Everyone was happy, laughing, and genuinely enjoying one another's company. There was no pressure, no awkwardness at all.

Why do I feel it important to share this part of the story? I want to show, once again, how wonderful the little (or big) moments of our lives will be (notice I did not say "can be") if we turn our will over to Heavenly Father. We think we can see everything. We think we can plan things out just perfectly. We can do neither. *He* can see everything we are missing. It's similar to when a child insists that the county fair is the most exciting place on earth, but you are about to introduce them to Disneyland. Heavenly Father has so many "Disneyland" moments that He is just waiting to surprise us with.

We think we can see everything. We think we can plan things out just perfectly. We can do neither. He can see everything we are missing.

I will never forget what my mom said to me in a phone call later than night. We had been chatting about the afternoon and how much fun it was. Then she said, "Dad said he had never seen you look more beautiful than you did today." I knew what he meant. It had nothing to do with my hair or makeup. It had everything to do with how genuinely happy I was in that moment. For a few hours, everything was right and perfect in my world. When we get to have those moments, we radiate light. We are completely at peace. Other people cannot help but take notice.

Unfortunately, as I mentioned before, another doubt was about to present itself. I was about to go from a really intense high to a terrifying low in about a day's time. And it proved to me that sometimes our faith in what we know is right is the only thing we have to hold onto, and that we can have peace amidst chaos if we do.

NINE

Faith vs. Fear: Who Wins?

*a*s that Sunday afternoon turned into evening, I eventually surrendered to the fact that I still had to drive back to Mesa so that I could be at work at 7 a.m. the following morning. Cameron would be staying in Show Low for a couple more weeks. It felt unnatural to be leaving him and it was harder than I had anticipated. Now that he was home and I could see him face to face, hold his hand, and kiss him, why would I be leaving him behind? He promised to call me after I got off work the next day so I immediately made that my focus and began counting down the hours until I could at least hear his voice again.

While I was driving, I replayed the entire glorious weekend in my mind. I tried to make every single detail permanent in my brain so I would never forget any pieces or any feelings. It was all just too good! And then that other doubt made its appearance: What if it all *was* too good? Too good to be true? As the night wore on and morning came, I continued to worry. What if it had all happened too fast? What if Cameron was uncomfortable with how quickly we had become an item? I even went so far as to worry that I had read the signs from him wrong and that maybe he wasn't really set on being with me! What if he wanted to date around to make sure I was the one he truly wanted to marry? It is truly fascinating where the human brain can take a person's emotions!

I was working at a preschool at the time and I got off work at 4 p.m. I was hoping my cell phone would ring at 4:01p.m., and that Cameron would be on the other end, ready to talk for hours and put every silly doubt I had been wrestling with out of my head for good. He didn't. I went home to my apartment and tried to occupy my mind while desperately waiting for his call. I had told my friend Kym all my doubts (we worked together at the preschool so she had to endure my craziness all day), and she had tried to assure me I was being completely irrational. By 7p.m. he still had not called and I was beside myself. At this point, I would not have been surprised if he called Kym and asked her to tell me it was over. I remember I was starting to annoy *myself* with these thoughts and doubts, so I made myself go to bed early, just to shut my brain off. I was a hot mess!

Within all the doubts and fears I was agonizing over, a quiet little voice kept trying to speak over all the noise in my head and my heart. "Didn't you already get your answer to this situation? Weren't you absolutely sure that you and Cameron would be married? Why are you worried? All of these doubts are unnecessary." That little voice was right. But my doubts were louder and seemed more real now without Cameron next to me. My faith was wavering. What if I had imagined that answer I had received? What if it was just what I had wanted to believe at the time?

Cameron finally called around 8 p.m., and although I was incredibly relieved to hear his voice, I feared what he might say. This one phone call could end the fantasy of our magical future together that I had built up in my head. I had left my cell phone with Kym in the other room in case he called while I was asleep. This was a call I couldn't afford to miss! I remember hearing her tell him, "I am so happy you finally called! Bethany was freaking out that you wouldn't call!" Cameron was completely confused when she handed me the phone, so I unloaded on him! I told him every single doubt that had tortured me for the past 24 hours. I apologized if things had moved too fast between us that weekend. I even told him I understood if he felt the need to date other girls so that he felt more confident about us (assuming he didn't find someone better).

After I got everything out of me, Cameron laughed a little, and then did what I had hoped he'd do at 4:01p.m. that day. He assured me that things were absolutely perfect between us. He had no desire to go out with any other girl--he was sure I was who he wanted to be with. He even went on to say how he wanted to move to do Mesa sooner, rather than stay in Show Low for another week like he had planned. He wanted us to be together as much as I did. When we hung up later that night, I was on cloud nine! Once again, all was right with my world!

A little while later though, a phrase popped into my mind, "Oh ye of little faith..." How had I almost completely discounted an answer I had received from Heavenly Father? How had I lost trust in Him in my "time of need?" After talking with Cameron, all my doubts now seemed so silly and irrational. I was at peace again. And then I realized, Heavenly Father had given me that answer, that tender mercy, while I was still on my mission so that I wouldn't have to doubt in these moments when Cameron and I were apart. When that very first doubt appeared, my response should have been to remind myself, "You got your answer. Focus on the answer you received. Do not entertain these nonsensical doubts." Heavenly Father wants us to be happy. We know this life is meant to be filled with obstacles, trials, and other opportunities for growth. But even while we are experiencing those hardships, we can have peace. It comes down to what we choose to focus on. It has been said that faith and fear cannot exist together. In this moment, I had chosen to focus on the fear and doubts. I had chosen to focus on how all my happiness (as I saw it) could end in an instant. I let my peace go. It was not taken from me. I surrendered it.

When we become parents, we are given an opportunity to understand just a little more of how Heavenly Father must feel about each of us. How often do we try to convince our children to trust us in a moment of irrational (or sometimes even rational) fear? Just last week, I took our daughters to the dentist for a routine checkup and cleaning. My older daughter is old enough to understand that this process is generally pain free. But my younger daughter isn't yet fully convinced. I could feel her fear and worry as she repeatedly asked "What do they do? They take pictures of my teeth, right? And they brush them just like me?" If she could have just trusted what I was telling her, she would have been able to let go of any fear or worry, and had peace.

It takes faith to remember that Heavenly Father sees the whole picture. Not only does He know how to help us get through whatever difficulty we are facing, He is also able to help us feel peace while we are in the midst of chaos. He is able to remind us that everything happens for a reason and that one day, we will not only understand why we experienced that trial, but we will be grateful for the lessons we learned while suffering through. We will realize that now, having gone though that difficult time, we are better equipped for the trials we have not yet encountered. We are stronger, we are more faithful. We know, with absolute certainty, that Heavenly Father is there to help us cope and to bring us peace.

TEN

Learning to Adapt to Life's Curve Balls

*C*ameron and I got engaged about one month after he returned from his mission! Hey, when you know, you know! Late one night, we were talking in the living room of his apartment. We were discussing the future in general, and then more specifically, our future together. I think Cameron said something like "So when would you want to get married?" We both knew we were headed in that direction, so this question was not a big surprise. It was still March, so I replied, "Probably sometime this summer?" We both got excited that we were finally making these plans and it was feeling more real. He officially proposed on April 8, 2002 and we eventually set our wedding date for July 6, 2002.

I was surprised by how carefree I felt during the wedding and reception planning. As an admitted control freak, I thought I would surely become one of those "bridezillas" you hear about. But my focus growing up had always been getting married, not planning the wedding. Sure, I had colors that I'd planned to use in the decorating, but I didn't dream about my wedding dress or even care about what the cake looked or tasted like. I had turned the planning over to my mom and honestly, I'm pretty sure I frustrated her throughout my engagement because I *wasn't* more involved in the details and decisions.

My focus at the time though, was on spending as much time as possible with Cameron. After becoming so close through letters, it was such a different experience being together and I didn't want to miss a second of it if I didn't have to.

Our families were thrown quite a huge curve ball during our engagement. Just two weeks before our wedding, I was in Flagstaff for my bridal shower. Cameron's mom and sister had also driven to Flagstaff to attend. Unfortunately, at this same time a huge wildfire called the Rodeo-Chedeski fire, had begun near Show Low and after the bridal shower had ended and we had unloaded all the gifts at my parents' home, we got word that the residents of Show Low were being encouraged to evacuate their homes. It wasn't long until the decision was made that Cameron's family would spend that time away from their home at my parents' house. Cameron's aunt and three children had also arrived from Alaska for our wedding so they came to stay, too. It was quite a packed house!

Looking back, that time was such a blessing for both of our families. Anyone who knows my mom, knows what an amazing cook she is and how much she loves to host people. This unplanned event was right up her alley! Aside from the immense stress of the unknown effects the fire would have on their home, Cameron's family was able to be comfortable and well fed. It was also a major bonding opportunity for all of us. We have since spent many holidays all together and we have even traveled on vacations together. Our parents are great friends now, and Cameron and I continually acknowledge how blessed we are to have families that truly enjoy being together.

Thankfully, the Rodeo-Chedeski fire was contained one day before our wedding. We left for our honeymoon the day of our wedding, so our receptions were scheduled for the following weekend. We had the first reception in Flagstaff on Friday evening and the other on Saturday night in Show Low at Fool Hollow Lake. We were told repeatedly that night and in the coming days how grateful people were to have a happy, fun reason to get together after the trauma the forest fire had brought to Show Low. I watch the video of that reception now and I can see the relief and happiness on the faces of our friends and family who lived in Show Low at that time. They had truly been through a horrific event and now they could finally take a breath, relax, smile, and dance.

As for Cameron and I, our life together was just beginning. And, boy, was it busy! Cameron was apprenticing as an appraiser during the day and taking classes needed for his license at night. I was also working all day at a different preschool and had enrolled at Pima Medical Institute in their night program to acquire my medical assistant front office certification. Although we hardly saw each other during the week, this was also a time that brought one of my favorite memories. I always got off work around 4p.m. and my class didn't start until 7 p.m. I would drive home after work, cook dinner, then drive to Cameron's office and we would have dinner together at a little picnic table behind his office complex. It was the perfect opportunity for us to connect during the day and to recharge for our classes each evening.

I had been hesitant to enroll in classes again. My college experience at Dixie had left me feeling defeated. I had felt stupid, inadequate and basically like a failure. Why would I want to sign up for the type of "fun" again? I knew I needed some type of degree or certification though. My mom had suggested trying a trade school. She explained that maybe having only one subject to focus on might be easier for me. Well, turns out she was right! I loved it! All the medical terminology made complete sense to me and I got A's through the whole program. I *wasn't* stupid! I was able to use that certification to get a full-time job in a medical office close by. While I was thrilled to finally have some self-confidence back, I wouldn't learn until many years later what my issues with school really were.

Cameron and I had discussed the idea of trying to have a child and we had originally agreed to wait for a year before starting that journey. But about five months into our marriage, a good friend of mine had her first baby. Cameron and I were at the hospital while she was in labor. We waited anxiously in the waiting room and shortly after she delivered her baby girl, we were invited in to meet her. It was amazing! To say it made us baby hungry would be a major understatement! We left that hospital and decided we couldn't wait seven more months to begin trying to have a baby. Besides, we had heard that it could take a few months for it to actually happen. We had no idea that we were opening the door to one of the most grueling and painful phases of our married life.

ELEVEN

Infertility: Anger, Jealousy, Hope, Oh My!

*W*hen I was younger, the two major tasks on my "to do" list were: first, get married, and second, have children. Honestly, anything other than that was extra credit, in my opinion. The first task had taken longer than I would have planned, had it really been up to me. It had been frustrating for me to have to wait so long for Cameron to come along so I could finally continue moving forward with my life. I naively thought that *now* my life would play out according to my own personal script. I couldn't create my husband--I had to wait for him to arrive. But I could create my children. Right?

We weren't too surprised or concerned when we didn't become pregnant in the first few months of trying. After six months, we started to consider that maybe there was a problem, but we had been told that most doctors won't begin testing or offer different methods until after a couple had tried for a full year.

There was a specific worry that I had carried with me since my teen years. That worry was that I would either struggle to have biological children or not be able to have them at all. My older sister and I have very similar physical and chemical issues. I had watched her struggle to become pregnant at age 20. Despite the endometriosis that made conceiving almost impossible, she was eventually blessed with two beautiful daughters, but then was forced to undergo a full hysterectomy, removing any possibility of bearing more children. Due to this family history, along with a history of extremely painful monthly cycles, my gynecologist suggested I go in for a laparoscopic exploratory surgery to diagnose and treat, or rule out, endometriosis. He did, in fact, find endometriosis growing inside, but didn't see it as a large enough problem to hinder pregnancy. So even with this new information, we were still basically at square one.

After we completed that first year of trying with no success, we sought help. At first, I was given Clomid by my gynecologist to take for a few months. I was warned that there was a risk of becoming pregnant with twins on Clomid, but I assured them that we would be thrilled if that risk actually transpired! I will never forget the horrible hot flashes I endured while taking Clomid. I recall riding in the back seat of my in-law's car, driving down the road in Show Low in the middle of winter. I was so miserable that I actually rolled the window down and stuck my head out the window like a dog, in an attempt to cool myself down! Still, this misery was worth every second if it resulted in a baby...or two! But alas, it did not.

We decided to get serious about this endeavor and we enlisted the help of a reproductive specialist (fertility doctor). One tender mercy we had been blessed with was Cameron's income. We honestly never went through the "poor newlywed phase." Money was great from the beginning of his profession as a real estate appraiser. This was such a big blessing, as our insurance company did not cover fertility treatment. Any testing or procedures were paid for out of pocket.

Cameron and I were both tested to rule out any significant issues that might be hindering the process. Our results both came back normal, which was both a relief and frustrating at the same time. While we were relieved to know that neither of us were the problem, we were now left to wonder why it wasn't happening. Our doctor suggested we try up to four months of IUI (intrauterine insemination) attempts. These were the cheapest form of fertility treatment and since we both showed no signs of infertility individually; our chances were good that this would do the trick. For the next three months, all we ended up with were negative pregnancy tests. By this point, I was ready to pull out the big guns. As we sat in our doctor's office discussing the latest negative IUI attempt, I broke down and told him I was not willing to do this for another month. I was ready to move on to in vitro fertilization. I was emotionally exhausted with the idea of trying yet another IUI and I was ready to begin the method that would be our last-ditch effort to bring a biological child into this world.

We had been struggling through infertility for a little over two years at this point and I have not yet mentioned how this trial was affecting us individually or as a couple. To this day, I still say that I would not wish infertility on my worst enemy. It is a brutally emotional mind game that can turn a woman into somebody even she doesn't recognize or like. I insist on being open and honest with people about how I handled this trial, not to show how hard it was for me, but to assure other women who are enduring infertility that the thoughts and feelings they are experiencing are normal and do not make them a bad person.

I experienced a wide range of emotions during these years. I remember the hope I would somehow conjure up each new month, just knowing *this* would be the month it worked. I would count out the months to see when our baby would be born. I would let myself think of cute, creative ways we would announce the pregnancy to our families. I can still feel the immense despair that would overcome me as I eagerly watched a pregnancy test that was refusing to produce that second pink line. You would think you'd get used to seeing a negative test, but you never do. It hits just as hard every single month. In just a minute's time, all those hopes I'd had were thrown on the ground and stomped on.

I was incredibly jealous of any pregnant woman that crossed my path. I didn't care if they were so miserably sick that they could hardly function. I didn't care if they were placed on bedrest for half of their pregnancy because they had a high-risk pregnancy. I didn't care if it was an unplanned pregnancy that they were struggling to accept as part of their plan. All I knew or cared about was that they had a baby in their belly. In my eyes, they were all so incredibly lucky. They had what I wanted most.

Anger was a faithful companion to me. I was angry at Heavenly Father. I was trying to fulfill the calling of being a mother, a calling that I had been taught that I should pursue. This was a righteous desire. Hadn't I earned this? Hadn't I served a mission? Hadn't we been sealed in the temple? I felt I had done my part. Why were other women and even young girls being blessed with this beautiful gift that they were not even planning for, that some of them didn't even want?

I was irrationally angry at any woman I knew that became pregnant. Especially those women that only tried for one or two months. They hadn't done their time. It wasn't fair. I remember clearly how it felt to hear someone say, "I'm pregnant!" or "She's pregnant!" I can only compare it to what it must feel like to be punched in the stomach. It feels like the air has been knocked out of you. One of the hardest things to do, something I don't feel I ever was able to successfully pull off, was smiling genuinely and saying, "Congratulations!" As soon as I learned someone was pregnant, she was off my list as far as I was concerned.

At one point, I began meeting with a counselor to help me cope with all my emotions. She taught me something that changed the way I view anger. After I had unloaded and told her how angry I was, she informed me that anger is a "cover-up emotion." Anger covers a true emotion. In that moment, I realized the emotion that I was covering up. The true emotion I was feeling was incredible sadness. But why was I covering it up? There were a few reasons. First, there wasn't time to be sad. If I began to cry each time I wanted to, I would have been a bawling mess! I would have cried at work multiple times a week, I would have cried in grocery stores and at parties. Now, I'm not saying I never cried. Believe me, it would have served me well to buy stock in Kleenex! I remember being caught off guard when a couple blessed their baby in church on a Sunday that isn't normally designated for baby blessings. I literally sobbed out loud and had to get up and rush out during the blessing. I preferred to cry in private. Therefore, in order to hold it together in public, I would employ my trusty friend, anger. Focusing on how angry I was helped to keep the tears at bay.

Anger was a faithful companion to me. I was angry at Heavenly Father. I was trying to fulfill the calling of being a mother, a calling that I had been taught that I should pursue. This was a righteous desire. Hadn't I earned this? Hadn't I served a mission? Hadn't we been sealed in the temple? I felt I had done my part.

Another reason I covered up my sadness was for the benefit of other people. It's a little awkward when someone announces exciting news and you burst into tears. Talk about raining on somebody's parade! I worried that I would not only ruin their moment of joy, but that I would also "steal their thunder" and turn the focus to myself. In order to avoid both scenarios, I would think about how unfair it was that they were pregnant. Hadn't they only been married for three months? Did they seriously get pregnant the first month they tried? I am embarrassed to admit that I even had the audacity to think that Heavenly Father must not think those women were very strong. They could never handle infertility. They aren't as strong as I am. Because, obviously, I was handling this trial with flying colors (sarcasm implied)!

These thoughts led to the other emotion that plagued me: guilt. Now, I'm a person that feels guilt without the help of anyone else! I tell people that giving me a guilt trip is essentially "hitting below the belt." It really isn't fair. The sadness I felt was inevitable and placed on me against my will. Although I was somewhat in survival mode and using anger was the only way I knew how to cope, I always felt guilty afterward. I felt like such a horrible human being. What kind of monster is mad at someone for creating life? What kind of jerk thinks that someone is weak because they were able to conceive quickly and somewhat easily? I was turning into an awful person and the guilt I felt was over-powering me.

I also felt guilt that I believe a lot of women who experience infertility can relate to. Even though there were tests that proved that I was not the reason we weren't getting pregnant, I felt guilty that I was not able to make Cameron a dad. I felt like a failure as a woman. I mean, he had been able to fulfill his "role" as the provider for our family. I was supposed to "provide" the children, and I had failed to do so. There were many times, mainly at night, when I was in my lowest of emotional lows, that I would beg Cameron to leave me and go marry a woman who could make him a dad. Thankfully, he was smart enough to acknowledge that maybe I wasn't being completely rational and he would assure me repeatedly that he would have still married me even if he would have known we may never have kids.

Going through infertility as a couple is extremely tough. Did you know that the divorce rate for couples who experience infertility is 75%? Infertility seems to place a looming, dark cloud over your relationship. You are surrounded by friends and family who are able to grow their own families. You watch with envy as they bring a child into this world and you can't help but acknowledge the new level of love and closeness that couple now shares, having gone through something so hard, but so beautiful. As the days, months, and sometimes even years pass by, you wonder if you will ever experience the same things those other couples do.

As a woman, I obviously cannot speak for men on this topic, but watching how Cameron navigated through this trial, he didn't seem to feel the same level of devastation as I did. For men, generally their role is to be the provider. Our inability to have children did not affect his role. Now, I am not implying that he didn't long for children as much as I did, but he was able to continue his daily routine and his role in this world and in our family without feeling as though something was missing from his life. Even if we had kids, he would continue to get up every day and go to work. Not too much would change for him.

Cameron is also a very positive, optimistic person by nature. He does not see the value in wallowing in sadness or self-pity. He is very rarely angry and when he is, it literally lasts for a few minutes. These qualities are a major reason I married Cameron. While he was extremely understanding, sympathetic, and loving towards me, he never cried or got angry about our situation. I was fine with the way he handled this, until something my friend said made me think differently.

We had some close friends, another couple, going through infertility at the same time as us and after hearing her tell me how her husband had broken down crying about this hard trial we were all experiencing, I was surprised to realize I was jealous. He was just as upset as she was. This *was* a painful road to travel and her husband had validated that for her. I thought I wanted that from Cameron. This bothered me for quite a while until I realized that this thing I wanted from him, a show of emotion, sadness, pain, very easily would have destroyed me. I was already feeling guilt I had placed on myself for not being able to give Cameron children. Seeing him physically upset would have compounded that guilt a thousand times!

It was then that I began to understand how couples work. As we go through life, we take turns being the strong one in the relationship. At other times in our marriage, I had the opportunity to strengthen and encourage Cameron. I had helped calm his fears and reassured him of his abilities before he took his exam to become a licensed real estate appraiser. My inability to fulfill my role as a mother was extremely difficult and it affected every aspect and area of my life. Cameron knew this. Now it was his turn to be strong for me. He may have vented his frustrations and sadness during this trial to others, but he knew that putting that added pressure on me would only push me down further into the darkness I already felt. Cameron knew his job was to try everything he could think of to pull me from that darkness and over time, we came up with strategies to navigate through infertility so that it would not destroy us. For example, we always planned a trip for Mother's Day weekend. Even if it was just a staycation, we did our best to forget that it was a special holiday I was not yet privileged to be a part of (don't worry, we did call our mothers). In the church, it is customary to hold baby blessings on the first Sunday of the month, Fast Sunday. On those days, we would purposely show up late so as to miss those blessings that were so beautiful, and yet caused us so much pain. I would tell my friends that when they became pregnant, to please tell me in a text message or email. I knew how I would feel upon hearing that news, and if I could read it and absorb it on my own first, I could then respond honestly and positively, in my own time. Cameron and I also traveled a lot. We both love to travel, so we tried to take advantage of the "unwanted freedom" we had been given. Basically, anything that would take our minds off of what we desperately wanted, we were willing to try.

People often ask couples who are struggling to conceive if they've thought about adoption. This is a very stupid question, in my opinion (of course, we've thought about it!). We explored the adoption process, but never felt that it was the path we should embark on. I can honestly say that was the only time I have experienced the "stupor of thought" spoken about in the Book of Mormon. I don't mind filling out paperwork, sometimes I kind of enjoy it (weird, I know), but filling out those forms for the adoption agency was nearly impossible for me. It was almost as if the forms were in another language. It was so strange for me to not be able to complete something that could possibly bring us the one thing we wanted most. All I could think was that it must not be the right path for us.

My mother is a very faithful woman. During these years of heartache, I relied heavily on her faith. I know she struggled in her own way having to watch her daughter suffer through what she knew as a righteous desire. Many times, she would reassure me that she believed I would have children of my own one day. Not just children, but a daughter. I had to cling to her belief and hope to stay afloat.

TWELVE

Life Would Be Much Easier If We Could Just See the Future

*W*ith our doctor's approval, we moved forward with the in vitro fertilization process. The first step was what was called a "sono mock". This is like a "pretend embryo transfer" with a sonogram so that the doctor can see any reasons it may not work. This was a very routine process, but in my case, the doctor found a problem. He pointed to something on the screen inside my uterus and asked me, "Do you see that?" I did, and he explained what it was: a polyp. It was not supposed to be there. My uterus was literally collapsing around it and it needed to be removed. I assumed he meant we would remove it at his earliest convenience, but two days later, I was in surgery and the polyp was removed.

Now, this wasn't the only excitement in our lives at this time. My birthday was a few days prior to this sono mock, and Cameron had surprised me with an incredibly adorable little Brittany puppy we named Buster. I was so excited to finally have something to take care of. Buster filled a small portion of the void I was feeling of not having a child. I could be Buster's mom.

Well, just a couple days after we got Buster, he started acting different. He was lazier than a puppy should be, and he wasn't eating very much. We became concerned and decided to call the breeder Cameron had bought Buster from. She became almost hysterical as soon as she realized who she was talking to and explained that Buster's litter had gotten Parvovirus (parvo). Cameron had paid cash for Buster so she had no way to get in touch with us to warn us about the illness. She told us to get him to the animal hospital right away, but also informed us that two puppies from that litter had already passed away. We did as she said and sure enough, Buster had parvo. We were able to transfer and admit him to our veterinary clinic where they would monitor and care for him around the clock. As you can imagine, this was not cheap. We considered changing his name to Amex, as he was racking up quite the bill on our American Express card! We were willing to do whatever it took to heal Buster: he was like our first child. But even with this special care and monitoring, there was no guarantee Buster would survive.

I remember my dad calling to check on me during this time. He knew about Buster as well as the surgery. He asked how I was holding up and I let it all out. I told him how angry and baffled I was. Not only are we unable to have children, but we can't even have a dog? Does Heavenly Father just not want us to be happy at all? I explained how I couldn't believe all of this was happening to us, and all at the same time. My wise, caring father just listened and reassured me that he knew we would get through this rough patch. There wasn't much else he could say, and he couldn't fix our problems. All he could do was comfort me, but I was so grateful for that. To our joy and relief, Buster survived and after a week in the clinic we were able to bring our puppy home. We were a little family again.

At my follow up appointment with our doctor, we asked the doctor if the polyp he removed might have been causing the problem all along. He wasn't sure, but encouraged us to try conceiving on our own for a few months to find out.

After a month or two, my period was late. This was not totally uncommon for me, and I dreaded taking pregnancy tests by this point. But we had been given new hope after my surgery so I decided to take one. I didn't tell Cameron I was taking it though. There was no point in getting his hopes up as well. For the first time since we had begun trying to have a baby, I saw a positive result on a pregnancy test! There was no mistaking that second pink line! I was shocked and so happy! We had just gotten home from a trip and Cameron was driving home from picking up Buster, who my parents had kept while we were away. I had to go into work, so I texted him and told him to stop by my office on his way home since I had missed Buster and wanted to see him. When Cameron arrived, I went outside to our car and told him the good news. He was just as shocked as I was, but so incredibly happy. I told him that I had already called our fertility doctor's office and they had instructed me to go have bloodwork done on my lunch break to confirm the pregnancy, which I had done. It was finally happening for us! We decided not to tell anyone for now, as it was still very early in the pregnancy. We enjoyed our own little private news together.

Later that afternoon while still at work, I started to feel some cramping. I went to the bathroom, fearing the worst, and the worst was confirmed. I was not only bleeding, but also passed something that I knew had caused that positive pregnancy test. I knew I was no longer pregnant. I couldn't hold it together. I told my wonderfully kind and sensitive coworkers that I was not feeling good and needed to go home. Not long after I was safe in the privacy of my own bedroom, my phone rang. It was the nurse from our doctor's office. I answered it, and with more enthusiasm than I was expecting, she squealed, "You are, in fact pregnant!" She had received my bloodwork results from earlier in the day. That poor nurse had no idea what had transpired since then. I explained what had happened and I could immediately feel her embarrassment and sorrow for the extra salt in the wound she had unknowingly added. I assured her that not only was I not upset with her, I was touched that she would be so excited for me. And even though I was hurting, physically and emotionally, I reminded *her* of the silver lining: I had gotten pregnant. This was new territory for us! We now knew it could happen.

Some people might look at that entire situation and consider it such a cruel experience of nature. I did not. I was able to see it for the tender mercy it was. Yes, we had gone from very high to very low in a day's time, but we hadn't even had a chance to tell family. Nobody else knew, but us. Cameron and I were able to cope with that loss without a well-meaning and caring audience. While we were going through infertility I often said, "I just wish I could see the future to know if we were even going to have children. If I knew they would be coming at some point, I could relax." I believe this experience was Heavenly Father's gift to me. He was giving me a glimpse that I had hoped for. I knew my body could become pregnant. I had new hope!

A little over a year of trying on our own after the miscarriage, we decided to try in vitro fertilization again. I began the injections and medications. While I don't love getting poked with needles, that didn't bother me too much. What I didn't like I was having to time every little thing. It was all so clinical and cold, not to mention painful. The process and stress were taking a toll on our marriage and more issues were coming up that we needed to work on and resolve between us. They weren't major issues, just some things we weren't in agreement with. At one point, Cameron asked me, "Do you really think we should be bringing a child into all of this?" You might think I would have lost my mind and thrown a frying pan at him for saying that, but surprisingly, I knew he was right. We needed to be strong as a couple before we invited children into our family. In a shocking decision, we decided to quit the injections and medications right then.

Back when we had begun the in vitro process this time around, my mom cautiously told me that she and my dad felt strongly that they needed to go serve a mission. I agreed, not really under-standing her hesitation. Then she said, "I'm just so worried that you will get pregnant and have a baby while we are gone." I reminded her that we had been trying for over three years with no baby to show for it. There was a good chance no babies would be born while they were serving. I told her that she needed to follow that prompting and not worry about me. And I meant every word.

It is a major sacrifice for senior couples to leave their children and grandchildren to go serve missions. There are missed celebrations, they are far away when trouble arises, etc. But for all the sacri-fices, those couples and their families are promised blessings for their service. I can vouch for those blessings. About a month and a half after we quit the in vitro process, and shortly after my parents received their call to the Philippines Olongapo Mission, I saw my second positive pregnancy test! Only this time, I stayed pregnant!

I had been late again for a few weeks. I had already taken two pregnancy tests that both turned up negative. I decided this was the last test I was going to take. Whatever answer it gave me would be the final decision. I even bought one of those tests that actually says "pregnant" or "not pregnant" on it so I could be sure. It was a Sunday morning, and I remember sneaking out of bed and into the bathroom before Cameron woke up. Once again, I did not want him to get his hopes up, too. I sat in the bathroom with the door locked until the result showed itself. PREGNANT! I think I was more shocked with this positive result than the first one I got. I honestly thought, after two negative tests, that this would be my final negative result, just to drive that knife deeper into my heart. I had prepared myself for it this time, I was ready. It almost took a moment to convince myself that what I was seeing was real. As soon as I was convinced, I washed my hands and crept over to Cameron's side of the bed. I gently woke him up and as soon as his eyes were open, I held up the test. Once again, we celebrated!

You would assume that after our last experience with a positive result and then quickly losing it, that we might keep this secret to ourselves a little longer, in fear that it would end the same way. For some reason, this time it felt more real. We immediately called our family members and told them the wonderful news. There were lots of tears and happy squeals!

While pregnancy was not the glorious experience I had envisioned, I was grateful for every discomfort, moment of nausea, and swollen ankles, too! My parents left for their mission when I was about seven months pregnant. My mom's fear had come true-they would miss the birth of my first daughter. That's right, my mom was right about that, too. She had pictured me with a daughter and it was finally happening. I kept reassuring her that she needed to go. I joked that if she stayed home, Heavenly Father might take my baby back!

I went through 24 hours of labor, back labor I might add, before my daughter's heart rate began dropping with each contraction. I was dilated to 9 cm, but we knew we needed to get her out as quickly as possible. I remember being so worried as the nurses literally shook my big, swollen belly in an attempt to get her heart rate back to normal. An emergency c-section was decided upon, and we finally got to meet our beautiful Haylee Brynn. On September 28, 2007, I officially became a mom. Cameron was now a dad. We couldn't have been happier.

THIRTEEN

How Have I STILL Not Caught On?

*I*n the years we were trying to conceive, we had bought a big, beautiful two-story home that we believed we would live in forever and raise our kids to adulthood in. We had a pool built in the backyard. I loved to picture the prom pictures we would take on our staircase. Now we had our first baby and life was finally getting back on track and beginning to follow the script I had written. I should have known that it all seemed just a little too easy and comfortable.

While I was pregnant with Haylee, Cameron had started his own appraisal company. It was doing great and I loved the flexibility of his job. Well, a few months after Haylee was born the market began to tank. Cameron's work slowed almost to a complete stop. He picked up two newspaper routes just to keep some money coming in. He would dress up and go out all day trying to find business for his company, and then wake up around midnight and go roll and throw newspapers.

It didn't take long for us to realize it made more sense for us to give up our forever home. We couldn't afford it anymore. That was a tough decision to make, but we knew it was the right one. It never ceases to amaze me how Heavenly Father jumps in as soon as He can when we are trying our best to do the right thing. We put our home up for sale and only had one person come look at it. One person. We had finally agreed to go through with this sacrifice and now we couldn't even get rid of this home? But we did finally sell that home. And guess who bought it? That one woman who had come to see it.

We learned a great, but hard lesson during that time. Money had been great ever since Cameron began appraising. While we weren't spending money carelessly on things that we didn't need, we also weren't budgeting very well. Or at all. We learned that we needed to be more prepared for the future in case this downturn happened again. We realized that when we could buy a home again, we needed to only buy a home suitable for the family we had, nothing too extravagant. We were put through a crash course of money management.

After selling our home, we began renting a smaller home nearby. It was tough to downsize into a home that we knew we would not be in forever. We were blessed to be renting from good friends who gave us liberty to paint the walls so it would feel more like "our" home.

Even with this big change in our lives, we were happy. We had our little girl. We had a real family of our own. Haylee was quite possibly the easiest baby and toddler ever born! But since she was our first, and we had nothing to compare her to, we naively thought it was our incredible parenting that made her so great and easy. I hate to admit that while Haylee would be happily sitting in the grocery cart, entertaining herself with an old receipt I'd found in my purse, I would see other children in grocery stores throwing fits, or running wild and think to myself, "Do his parents teach him nothing? Do they just not care that he is annoying the rest of us?" I was so naive. I was finally able to be the mom I had always dreamed I'd be with Haylee. We made holiday crafts for each holiday, we baked cakes and frosted cookies together. We had play-dates all the time with friends and we could even take her to dinner with us at restaurants because she was so well-behaved. Once again, I should have known things were just a little too comfortable and easy. By this point in my life, I should have caught on to the pattern of the ups and downs I had experienced! I had no idea what our future held.

FOURTEEN

Some Lessons Take a Couple Rounds to Learn

*A*lthough it had taken us longer than expected to begin our family, Cameron and I did not want to have our children too close together. We felt that it would be best to wait until Haylee was around 18 months old to begin trying for another baby. Once again, I naively thought that all was right in my world at last, and that having children now would be a breeze. After all, Haylee had come naturally. In my mind, we would have no problems conceiving now.

Wrong. Ever heard of secondary infertility? That's what it is called when you have given birth to one or more children and then find yourself struggling to conceive again. I honestly couldn't believe it. I thought we were past this! Hadn't I learned the lessons I needed to learn? Hadn't we worked out the issues in our marriage already? It made no sense to me why we would be struggling to have a baby all over again. We decided that since Haylee had been conceived naturally, we would not try fertility treatments this time. Ultimately, we came to the conclusion that, like the saying goes, beggars cannot be choosers. We had been so blessed to have Haylee. Maybe one child was all we were going to be given. We *had* been blessed with a pretty special little girl!

After we had been trying to add to our family again for nearly two years, my mom was talking to me in my home about the possibility of her and my dad going on another mission within the next year. Again, she was worried about the possibility of missing another grandchild being born, and honestly, after what had happened with Haylee, she had more reason to worry. Just as before, I told her that she needed to do what was right for her and my dad and go serve. I reminded her that, once again, we had been trying for almost two years to no avail, and that it may not happen again for us at all. I remember we sort of joked about maybe if they served another mission, we would get another baby. But in all honesty, in my heart, I had very little hope of having another child. By the end of our conversation, she had decided that they would put their papers in to serve. Missions are a little different for senior couples. Sometimes they are able to be a little more selective about where they will serve. My parents had some friends that had been serving in a different mission in the Philippines than where they had served their first mission and had told my parents how badly they needed more senior couples there. They had asked my parents if they would choose to come serve in the Cebu temple. My parents agreed and the plan was that they would not leave for almost another year.

About a month after that conversation with my mom, I realized I was about two weeks late. That wasn't altogether odd for me, but I would be lying if I said I wasn't starting to have a tiny bit of hope. I had resigned to the fact that Haylee would be an only child. It made sense. She had such an independent, confident personality. She didn't need people to entertain her. She happily trotted off to nursery, preschool, and even dance practice all by herself. Sometimes I wondered if she even needed Cameron and I! Still, what if she was meant to have a little brother or sister? That made sense, too. She would not struggle with jealousy and I could envision her wanting to help take care of a baby.

One morning, after Cameron had left for work, I decided to take a pregnancy test just to put my mind at ease. I never told Cameron when I took those tests. I remember Haylee was sitting in her high chair eating her breakfast and watching cartoons. I went into the bathroom, took the test, and then set it on the counter. I walked back into the kitchen to tidy up a bit and after a few minutes snuck back to the bathroom to see the results. I had gone back to using the pregnancy tests that just show a second line if it's a positive result, and to my complete shock, there were two pink lines! I remember running out to the kitchen, stopping, and just staring at Haylee with the most shocked look on my face! She was probably thinking her mommy was losing her mind! In one small moment, everything changed. She wasn't going to be an only child. It all began to sink in for me. All the memories, good and bad, from my pregnancy with Haylee. Would she have a little brother or sister? Where would we put another child in this house we had downsized to?

After ten or fifteen minutes of processing all the different thoughts that were flying through my mind, it finally hit me. I'm somewhat embarrassed to admit that it took me that long to realize what I believe had happened to us for a second time. My parents had committed to serving another mission...and here I was, pregnant with another long-awaited baby. I've said it many times before, I don't believe in coincidences. Especially not when it comes to Heavenly Father. I believe He keeps His promises to us when we do what He asks us to do. I know that my parents wanted another baby for us just as much as we did. Even still, I almost couldn't believe it. It was truly amazing to me that He had blessed us in the same way He had before. One of my favorite quotes is, "You can live as though nothing is a miracle, or as though everything is a miracle." I choose to believe the latter. Of course, thinking about my parents' mission led me to quickly do the math in my head. They would still be home when this baby was due! This time it was even better than before!

I'm somewhat embarrassed to admit that it took me that long to realize what I believe had happened to us for a second time. My parents had committed to serving another mission...and here I was, pregnant with another long-awaited baby. I've said it many times before, I don't believe in coincidences. Especially not when it comes to Heavenly Father. I believe He keeps His promises to us when we do what He asks us to do.

About five months later we found out that we were having another little girl. I'll admit, this surprised me. In my "script," it made sense that we would have a boy. After all, we already had a girl, so now we need a boy, right? I should have learned by this point in my life that things would most likely happen opposite of what I had planned! I am quite the slow learner. One evening, while Cameron and I sat watching television, we heard the name Jori. It immediately stuck out to me. We had not yet decided on a first name for our second daughter, but we had decided her middle name would be Lynn, the same as my middle name. Cameron said he liked the name Jori, but I worried that it might be too "different", so I texted my mom. I knew she would be honest with me. She agreed that yes, it was a little different, but not too crazy and she liked it. It was settled. Our baby had a name: Jori Lynn.

FIFTEEN

Heavenly Father Really Does Want Us To Be Happy

*A*ny woman who has more than one child will tell you that they are each completely different. Looks, personality, spirit, etc. This was no different in our case! When Haylee was born, she looked completely like her dad. She was beautiful with his olive skin. She didn't have very much hair at birth, but what little hair she did have was light and laid flat on her head. She looked nothing like what I was expecting! I had been born with a full head of thick, dark hair and light skin and I guess I expected her to look the same. If Haylee hadn't resembled Cameron so much, I might have wondered if she was really mine!

Since I had needed an emergency c-section with Haylee, my doctor recommended we have a scheduled c-section to deliver Jori. That was a control freak's dream! I got to choose her birthday! We drove to the hospital on the morning of July 8, 2011 and within a couple hours, Jori Lynn was delivered. I still remember how relaxed it felt in the room, with music playing on the radio while we chatted with the doctors and nurses just before she was born. I'll never forget the song that was playing when she was delivered. It was Over the Rainbow by Israel Kamakawiwo'ole--one of my favorite songs.

The second I laid my eyes on her, I knowingly stated, "*There* she is!" What I meant by this, was here was that chubby little girl with a full head of dark hair I had been expecting! I recognized her. She was mine. While Haylee Brynn had been all Comerford, Jori Lynn was all Kimberlin (my maiden name). And while they were both beautiful babies, they couldn't have been more opposite in the way they looked!

It was so wonderful to have my parents at the hospital when Jori was born. I'm sure my mom was having flashbacks of me as a baby when she looked at and held Jori. All babies are miracles, but I am biased in believing that our two daughters are even more special miracles. They are answers to prayers and blessings for service and sacrifice. They are proof that Heavenly Father not only exists, but that He loves us and wants to give us the righteous desires of our hearts.

Cameron and I got very lucky to have two babies who both began sleeping through the night around two months old. I really don't do well with little sleep, so I believe this was a major tender mercy. Maybe more for Cameron than for me! After having Haylee, who had been a dream baby, I was sure that we would have our work cut out for us with this second little girl. We were pleasantly surprised at how easygoing Jori was. I think the only difference I can recall is that I would joke about how it seemed Jori would wake up angry that she wasn't already eating! As soon as her eyes opened, it was feeding time and she made sure you knew it! To be honest, she's still that way today!

Jori's "room" was really our home office. We were planning to move before she turned one, so we made no attempt to create a real nursery for her. I had been right about Haylee-she never showed any signs of jealousy and she loved helping take care of Jori. Although we had had to try longer than expected to have Jori, the age gap of almost four years between the girls was really nice. Haylee was potty trained and capable of so much more at that age. Haylee loved to entertain Jori. She would lay on the floor with her and read books to her, sing songs, and do anything she could think of to try to make Jori laugh. And Jori adored her big sister! Haylee could get laughs out of Jori that we couldn't. She would get so excited whenever Haylee came near her.

We were living in Mesa when Jori was born, but we decided that when we bought our next house, we wanted it to be in Gilbert. We felt drawn to Gilbert just by appearance alone, but we had also heard wonderful things about their school system. We had good friends who had a son with autism and they moved from Mesa to Gilbert because of the great special needs program within the Gilbert school district. While that didn't apply to us, we still knew we wanted our kids to go to school in Gilbert.

It wasn't long after we began searching for a home to buy that we found "the one." It not only had a big backyard for the girls to play in, but it also had a pool. The girls could be out back year-round! We immediately fell in love with our ward and neighborhood. We knew without a doubt that we had found our place.

SIXTEEN

Sometimes All You Need to Do Is Ask

*A*s Jori got a little older, we started to see just how different she was from Haylee. While Haylee had been fairly calm, obedient, and content, Jori was loud, hyper, physical, and well, destructive. We often joked that we had, in fact, gotten our rough and tumble boy! Jori loved to wrestle, climb, push, pull, throw, etc. She also threw major fits like we had never seen before. Sometimes she would get so angry she would bite or scratch herself in an attempt to release her frustration.

When I took her to the pediatrician for her 18-month well check, I explained my concern that Jori still was not saying any real words. She babbled a lot and she had her own version of words that *we* had learned, but nobody outside our home could understand her. Her doctor recommended early intervention speech therapy. We also discussed how some of her tantrums and anger might be related to the fact that she was unable to communicate. Delayed speech definitely ran in my side of the family, so this wasn't a major concern for us. A short time later, Jori had tubes put in her ears as a result of multiple ear infections. We had hopes that this might help her speech as well.

By the time Jori was three years old, her speech had not improved much at all and her behavior had gotten worse. We couldn't take our eyes off of her for a second. It was as if her brain never stopped and if there was something she wasn't supposed to get into, you could almost guarantee she would find a way to do just that. Jori had obviously grown as well, so her power to destroy things was greater. She had even kicked a hole in her bedroom after being sent there for a time-out.

Jori had qualified for preschool at the elementary school Haylee attended, due to her speech issues. It was around that time that we started to notice something interesting. People-adults and children alike-were drawn to Jori. Although it seemed she was physically unable to keep her hands to herself, and sometimes she would push another child or squeeze a child a little too tight, she always had friends. When we would apologize profusely to her teachers, fearing that they would tire of her and consider removing her from their class, we were shocked to find the exact opposite. They adored Jori! I remember sitting at Jori's parent teacher conference with her preschool teacher. After informing me of all the good, but also the negative behaviors Jori had shown in her class, she went on to tell me how much she loved Jori. I'll never forget when she said to me "I know she's your child, but she's my baby."

Now, I had worked in preschools. I had dealt with some pretty tough kids in my time. I remember wishing, maybe sometimes even praying, that the parents of those kids would move their child to another preschool! After some of the notes from school we had received about Jori's behavior, I was sure her teachers felt the same as I had. But that was never the case. Not only were they not exhausted with her behavior, they loved having her in their class.

At home, it wasn't as happy. We quickly realized how wrong we had been to think we had any part in what an easy, well-behaved child Haylee been. None of our "amazing parenting skills" were having any effect on Jori's behavior. She honestly couldn't care less about following rules or doing what we wanted. We dreaded taking her to stores, restaurants, or the mall. Even if we got lucky and she behaved while we were there, it would almost always end in a major tantrum, that would attract stares from everyone nearby. This was incredibly hard for someone like myself, who had naively prided myself on being such a wonderful parent with my perfect child to show for it. I remember how I had judged those poor parents whose kids were throwing fits in the store. I was now one of them. I was being humbled very quickly.

It wasn't uncommon for me to feel defeated by the time bedtime rolled around each night. Most days the report from her teacher included how she had hurt another child or wasn't able to follow the rules that day. After school, she would go what felt like a million miles an hour around the house until it was time for bed. She would get into things she shouldn't have, she would do things without thinking that could have gotten her hurt, she would throw major tantrums if she was told "no," and she was just continuously moving from room to room, which meant I was moving from room to room with her. It was simply exhausting.

I will never forget the first big tender mercy we received with Jori's behavior. It had been a particularly rough day with her and I was way past feeling defeated. I was ready to give up altogether. We were saying prayers with the girls before they went to bed and in our family prayer I had asked that we could figure out how to help Jori behave better. As Cameron and I settled onto the couch to watch television, which we did every night, I turned on the latest episode of a series we had recorded called "Our America" with Lisa Ling. I remember Cameron questioning my choice that night. "Don't you want to watch something a little lighter and funnier tonight?" At that point, I felt like I couldn't even think straight! I just needed noise on, I didn't really care what it was about.

That episode "just happened" to be about ADHD (attention deficit hyperactivity disorder) in children. It wasn't long into the show, maybe five minutes, that I paused the tv and Cameron and I just looked at each other. They were showing a young boy, around 9 years old, whose mom was trying desperately to get him to do his homework. It was exhausting to watch! Not only was the boy not interested in doing his homework, it seemed that he couldn't even sit still in his seat, let alone focus on a math problem. It was like we were watching an older version of Jori!

We sat up straighter and paid more attention to the different families they interviewed on the show. They showed that same boy from the beginning doing an evaluation for ADHD. They first had him sit down and take a "test" with the woman evaluating him. The boy didn't know the mirror on the wall was a window his parents, and the cameras, could see in through. He was fidgeting with his hands and feet and looking all around the room, unable to focus on the evaluator. He scored fairly low on the test. Afterward, they had him go to lunch with his parents, take a medication prescribed for ADHD, and return to take the same test once more, this time medicated.

It was nothing short of fascinating! He was now able to sit still, focus on the woman giving the test, and give correct answers. He scored much higher this time, almost perfectly. His parents were in tears behind the glass. They were finally seeing the potential they knew had been hiding in their son. And for the first time in a very long time, we had hope for Jori. Little did I know, I was also about to understand even more about myself as we continued watching.

Part of the reason Lisa Ling had been interested in learning more about ADHD is because she wondered if she had it herself. When she went to be evaluated, she was asked several questions about her childhood and how she had performed in school. I remembered Lisa from her days at Channel One when I was in high school. For all I knew, she had gone to Harvard and graduated at the top of her class! She seemed extremely smart to me. But as she answered the questions, I felt like she was describing my own experience with school! She spoke about not doing well in classes she was not interested in. I, myself, had failed physics in high school because I didn't understand it and was not interested in it at all. Lisa went on to talk about dropping out of college. I was shocked! She talked about how she had done very well in classes she was interested in so she knew she wasn't dumb. At the end of the evaluation, she was diagnosed with ADD (attention deficit disorder).

I couldn't believe it. In one hour, I had been given answers not only for Jori, but for myself. I thought back to how I had felt when I dropped out of college. I had felt so stupid. I had failed at college. But then I thought about how well I had done at Pima Medical Institute. It hadn't made sense back then how I could fail at one type of schooling and excel at another.

This would be a perfect opportunity for someone to say that it was just a coincidence that we had watched that show that evening. You know what I will say though. Heavenly Father had answered my prayer. To be completely honest, that may have been the first time I had prayed to know how to help Jori. Even after all the experiences I had had and answers I had received in my life, as a control freak, I was so used to trying to figure out my own problems and find my own answers. All I had to do was ask Heavenly Father. He always has the answers, but He will not force His will. We have to ask Him.

Beginning that night, I learned everything I could about ADHD. I learned that when a child is diagnosed with ADHD or ADD, one or both of the parents is almost always diagnosed as well. That was the case for Jori and I, I just didn't have the hyperactivity factor that she did. Our pediatrician referred us to an amazing pediatric behavioral specialist to have Jori evaluated. Before her appointment, the behavioral specialist emailed me questionnaires to fill out about Jori. Upon receiving those answers, he would then send me another questionnaire with different questions. With all those answers I had sent, he had Jori figured out after about five minutes with her. She did, in fact, have ADHD. She was also diagnosed with Sensory Processing Disorder, which explained her need to climb, push, pull, hit, etc. Just when we thought the appointment had gone as well as we could have hoped, this doctor asked, "Have you ever heard of Childhood Apraxia of Speech?"

SEVENTEEN

But...why ME?!

J was stunned. As the behavioral specialist described apraxia to us, it was like he'd known Jori since she was nine months old. He explained that apraxia of speech is a neurological disorder, and that a child affected with it understands everything that is said to them, and they know what they want to say, but the connection between their brain and their mouth is too weak for them to say words correctly. These children usually need intense speech therapy specific to apraxia to learn to speak better. He suggested we have her evaluated by a speech and language pathologist to be sure, which we did.

That evaluation lasted over an hour and ended in an obvious diagnosis of Childhood Apraxia of Speech (CAS) and a new schedule of speech therapy appointments twice a week. I remember crying as I drove home with Jori in the backseat. I felt so overwhelmed. When she was diagnosed with ADHD and sensory processing disorder, I felt like we could cope well with those. I could name people with ADHD who had grown into amazing adults. I couldn't do that with CAS. This was new territory. We had no idea when, or if, she would ever speak normally.

Looking back now, that was a pretty dark time for me. I was driving Jori 20 minutes each way to speech therapy twice a week, as well as music therapy and occupational therapy once a week each. During these drives, she often threw fits in the backseat, scratching or biting herself or throwing her sippy cup at my head in anger. I felt trapped in a routine that I had not ever expected, or wanted, for that matter. I was seeing other moms set up playdates that we were invited to, but I knew we couldn't attend because Jori would go into fight or flight mode if there happened to be a dog or even a fly in the room. Fireworks displays were avoided because, if not, it ended in chaos as Jori would be taken over by terror. It was hard to invite friends over to play that were Jori's age because they couldn't understand her. Not to mention, the fact that she was so far behind where she should be would be in my face in the form of another cute little girl. I couldn't help but wonder about Jori's future, which was never a good idea. It was easy to become overwhelmed with the not-so-glamorous possibilities we might face down the road. It was much harder to imagine any sort of light at the end of this tunnel.

As I had done at other points in my life, I longed for Heavenly Father to grant me just a momentary glimpse into what the future with Jori would look like. I knew I didn't need to see every aspect, but I thought just a peek might calm my worried mind. It was during this dark time that I learned one way Heavenly Father helps us through our trials. While He can't always save us from the trial, He can teach us about the purpose of the specific trial and our ability to eventually overcome it. He knows us better than anyone, better than we know ourselves. He was about to help me understand my role in Jori's life.

While He can't always save us from the trial, He can teach us about the purpose of the specific trial and our ability to eventually overcome it. He knows us better than anyone, better than we know ourselves. He was about to help me understand my role in Jori's life.

General Conference was approaching. I had often heard the suggestion to have a question in your mind that you'd like an answer to during conference weekend. I had my question ready. It was the same question I asked so many times before in moments of frustration with Jori or her issues. It was a question that flew off my tongue almost daily, in a rhetorical manner, not really expecting an answer. But at this point in my life, I needed the answer desperately if I had any chance of enduring the task that had been placed upon me.

Why am I her mom?

That was my question. That's what I needed to know. I wasn't asking in a way of complaint, like, "Why do I have to raise her?" but out of true curiosity (and maybe also some belief that there must have been a mix up somewhere!) as to why *Jori* was stuck with *me*. I had seen other special needs moms in my life. They resembled angels on earth. They were patient and kind, possessing what seemed to be a naturally happy disposition. That wasn't me! Why wasn't she sent to one of those soft, patient, competent moms? Why does she have a mom who loses patience within seconds? Why does she have a mom that yells and needs time away from her to just survive? It didn't seem fair to Jori. I needed to know.

We attempted to listen to the Saturday sessions, but Jori wasn't too captivated by the men in suits on the television. Sunday morning wasn't much better, as Jori was bored with more speakers and mom and dad trying hard to hear what they were saying. In between sessions on Sunday we decided to take the girls to the park to feed the ducks and get out some energy. It was a great family outing. That is, until it came time to leave the park.

Now, Cameron and I had an unspoken agreement about Jori. Since I was with her most of the day every day, she was more of Cameron's responsibility when we were all together. I had learned to back away and let him handle her because he is more patient of the two of us. This day was no exception. I walked behind with Haylee as he struggled to carry a very angry Jori to the car. She did not want to leave the park and she was determined to let everyone within a two-mile radius know that! Once we got to the car, Haylee and I got into our seats and waited as Jori did everything in her power to keep Cameron from buckling her into her car seat. After a minute or so, I calmly asked Cameron if he'd like me to try and help. He politely declined. After another minute or so, I realized we may never leave this park! I got out of my seat came around the car where Jori was flailing her arms and legs, while also flexing her body into an unbendable statue. Most parents of angry toddlers know this move well and are picturing it now. It was impossible to secure the buckle where it belonged between her legs with her in this position, and she knew it. But something almost magical happened as I came around Cameron and into Jori's view. As soon as she saw me and realized I would now be taking Cameron's place in this battle, she surrendered instantly. She still was not happy, but she seemed to understand that her efforts would be futile against me. I thought about that moment as we drove home.

We listened to the final session of General Conference and I can honestly say that I don't remember anyone explaining to me why I was Jori's mom. Some people might say (and I agree completely as I've shared in previous experiences), that often our answers come through the Holy Ghost whispering to us while we may be listening to a talk on a completely unrelated subject. Well, that didn't happen either. I had pretty much resigned to the fact that I didn't get to know the answer to my question at this point. While disappointed, I still knew Heavenly Father had His reasons and I had faith in whatever those reasons might be.

That evening, as Cameron began bath time (he bathed, I blow-dried hair afterward), Jori decided to put on her own "splash show" in the bathtub. I listened from the kitchen as Cameron tried to get her to stop splashing, which seemed to only make her want to splash more. I stayed in the kitchen, letting him handle the situation in the bathroom, until I remembered what had happened at the park. After thinking about it for a minute, I became curious. Was that just a fluke? Did she just become too tired to fight us? Or did it really have to do with me?

My curiosity took over and I headed to the bathroom, where the "splash show" seemed to have really gained excitement. I peeked in, where I saw Cameron kneeling next to the bathtub as Jori was happily ignoring any attempts he made to stop her from splashing. As I walked into the bathroom and stood behind Cameron, Jori froze. Her eyes met mine and it was as if she knew splash time was over without me saying a word. Was this really happening?

And then my question was answered: *This* is why you are her mom.

All this time, I had been so hard on myself, just sure that what Jori needed was a mom who was the complete opposite of me. In this moment, I realized I was exactly the mom Jori needed. While yelling as a parent is never really condoned, in Jori's unique situation, I had proven myself as the "alpha" in our home, which is exactly what she needed. All kids crave boundaries, regardless of how much they fight them. Boundaries create a feeling of safety for them, and when those boundaries are not clear or happen to move, children can feel unstable and lost. Jori seemed to have a tougher time recognizing her boundaries. She tried harder than most kids to test every boundary to see if it would move. While she may have succeeded with other people in her life, she never did with me and she had all but given up trying. When she threw fits and yelled, I yelled louder. Like I said before, yelling is not typically an effective method with most children, but with Jori, I sometimes joke that I "matched her level of crazy." Her tactics to get her way would not work with me.

Now, it would be easy for a person reading this to wonder if Jori feared me at all times. Ironically, I am the one she prefers when she goes into her fight or flight mode. I believe that because of our similar "highly emotional" personalities, she looks to me for reassurance in uncertain situations. While I would do anything to have the patience my husband possesses, and his even-tempered personality, I believe Jori feels that she can trust what she gets from me in the moment, emotionally speaking. To her, Dad is always calm and happy, even when something legitimately scary is happening. But if Mom is calm, then it must really be okay and I don't need to be worried. Yet another reason I *am* supposed to be her mom.

Along with finally having the answer to my question, I was also humbled as the Spirit reminded me that Heavenly Father does not make mistakes. Even without knowing the reason I was supposed to be Jori's mom, I should have been content with the knowledge that Heavenly Father knows what He's doing even when we don't understand. We should rely on our faith in Him until we receive the answers we seek.

Jori is a few years older now, and more well-behaved...most of the time. She saves her hardest behaviors for us at home, which I really do appreciate. I am still the "alpha" in our home, therefore I handle more of the challenging parenting moments with her than my husband does. We've discussed that he needs to remain the "nice, soft parent." She still tests him a lot more than she tests me, and it frustrates him, but we've accepted that this is just how it needs to be with Jori. Receiving my answer has actually given me a sense of pride in caring for her, a sense of real purpose in her life. I learned that sometimes the answers to our dilemmas aren't always to just be "soft and tender." Sometimes we are put in positions where Heavenly Father needs us to step up and be bold. He puts us in places where our specific personality is needed. As long as there is love behind our actions, we can know we are doing what He expects and desires of us.

I sometimes get asked if we wanted or tried to have more children. Growing up, I never really had a set number of children I hoped to have. After struggling again to conceive our second child, we realized that it may always take us longer to become pregnant. Honestly, I wasn't sure I wanted to go down that emotional road one more time, especially as I was only getting older and there was no guarantee it would happen again for us. We had been blessed with two beautiful daughters and I wanted to focus on them, not spend my time wishing for another child. Then, as Jori's issues began affecting our daily life, I realized adding to our family just wasn't a good idea. Jori required so much of my time and energy that I didn't see how it would be possible to do what was required of me with morning sickness and then with a baby in tow.

Another concern is one that is on my mind every day. Our older daughter sacrifices quite a bit with Jori as her little sister. Jori demands our attention a lot of the time and Haylee has to wait until we are able to focus on her. While I feel the need to be honest, I hate to admit that some days I don't have the energy or emotional stamina to give Haylee the positive attention she deserves. There are a lot of fun places and events I would love to take Haylee to, but I can't because it would be too difficult (or impossible) with Jori. Because we are aware of all Haylee has to sacrifice, even when she doesn't even realize it's a sacrifice, it's very important to Cameron and I that we make time for Haylee. We let her participate in activities that interest her, take her to do things without Jori so she has all of our attention, let her stay up later with us after Jori goes to bed, and so on. My biggest fear with Haylee is that she will one day resent us or her sister, or both, for the things she missed out on. We make it a point to praise Haylee as often as possible and we tell her all the time how lucky Jori is to have such a great big sister. I know Haylee was supposed to come to our family first. She truly loves Jori and enjoys her role as Jori's big sister.

EIGHTEEN

Some Goals May Take Longer to Achieve, But They DO Happen

*A*s I've mentioned before, ever since I was a young teenager, I planned on being a psychologist and/or counselor. I feel the most fulfillment when I am able to help someone in a tough situation, especially when it involves a relationship with someone else, such as a spouse or other family member. I feel like Heavenly Father has blessed me with the ability to put myself in another's shoes and see things clearly from their vantage point. I've had various opportunities to help friends and family members over the years and it has brought me so much happiness.

When Jori was still around four years old and going to preschool a couple days a week, I began researching different possibilities and methods to achieve this goal of becoming a counselor. Going back to college was not an option after the experience I had had there. I knew that wasn't my path. For a while, I felt like I was forced to accept the fact that I would never achieve this goal due to my inability to get through college. And yet, I couldn't quit thinking about it.

One day, while on social media, the older sister of one of our good friends posted that she had become a certified life coach. I felt incredible jealousy! That's what I wanted to do! I immediately messaged her, even though she and I had never really talked one-on-one before, and I asked how she had gone about her certification. She explained a little about it to me and while I felt hope about the possibility of being able to do the same, I knew it was not the right time for me. Even though I had a few free hours during the week now, I was still very overwhelmed with driving Jori to her different therapies and getting everything else taken care of in our home.

A couple years later, during a road trip, Cameron and I were discussing the topic of me getting a job. Both of our daughters were in school all day at this point, so it was a possibility. My husband owns his own business and sets his own schedule, which I love! I expressed how my only reservation about getting a job, was being tied down to a schedule. I had been spoiled with his flexibility. We didn't come to any kind of conclusion then and I just decided to think about it for the time being.

About a week later, as I sat in a movie theater with my older daughter, Haylee, waiting for the movie to begin, I received a message on my phone from that same friend I had messaged two years before about becoming a life coach. Her message said, "How serious were you about wanting to become a life coach?" I was completely caught off guard! I immediately responded that I was very serious, that it was what I had always wanted to do. She informed me that they were training new coaches and she wondered if I was interested in being trained. She gave me the details and I told her I would get back to her after discussing it with Cameron.

My mind was reeling. It was a good thing I had seen that movie once before, because I was completely distracted by what had just transpired and the possibilities that were awaiting me. Was this real life? Did someone actually just come to me and *ask* me if I was ready to begin doing what I'd always wanted to do? I said a silent prayer in that dark theater and thanked Heavenly Father. At this point in my life, I knew He helped to orchestrate the meaningful events in my life. I just couldn't believe how fast He made this one a reality!

Cameron and I talked about this opportunity later that evening and we both agreed it was what I needed to do. At the time, I looked at this venture as me finally being able to help more people. I had no idea how going through the training would help *me*, or the impact it would have on my life. The timing couldn't have been more perfect.

The company I was certified through is a faith-based life coaching company. This was a perfect fit for me because throughout my life, I had learned to look at my hard times (trials) and good times (blessings) spiritually. I couldn't deny the presence or hand of a loving Heavenly Father in my life. I knew this was also true for friends, family, and future clients. Going through the training is basically being coached yourself. I had to go through the exercises and thought-processes first, using my own trials, thoughts, and feelings, before I could help someone else experience them. It is hard for me to express the shift that happened in my mind going through these exercises. Not only did I learn how much more capable I am of achieving goals I set, and how much my attitude and perspective really do affect my happiness, but most importantly, I gained a stronger, more intimate relationship with my Savior, Jesus Christ than I had ever had before. I have never had difficulty believing He is real, but through this process, he became my biggest ally. He became *real* to me in my own life. I learned to depend on Him and share my trials with Him when they were too much for me to handle. That one lesson has made all the difference in my life. I saw its effectiveness firsthand shortly after becoming certified.

Our daughter Jori is in the special needs program at her elementary school. She has an IEP (Individual Education Plan) specific to her needs and abilities. Every year, we as her parents meet with her teachers and the school counselor to discuss the goals we had set previously for Jori and whether or not she achieved them. Many parents dread these meetings because it can become a battle between parents and teachers about who knows what is best for the child. That has never been the case for us, though. Jori is blessed with some of the most amazing, loving, patient, teachers I've ever met. I know they love her and truly want what is best for her.

Before Jori's scheduled IEP this year, we were mailed a copy of her goals and how she had scored to look over. It was a somber feeling for Cameron and I as we realized that there was little, if any, progress made. It can be a struggle for any parent when they see their child not progressing like other kids their age. Although, we had become somewhat familiar with that issue over the years with Jori, this was different. We were learning that as she was getting older, even though she was making progress in many areas, the gap between neurotypical children Jori's age and herself was getting wider. The purpose of the program Jori was in at this time was to eventually integrate these children fully into the regular school classes with their peers. We, along with her teachers, realized this will not happen for Jori. We were told of another program that would be a better fit for Jori, but it would be at a different elementary school. It hit us both pretty hard, almost like a punch to the stomach. Along with the shock, I hated the idea of moving Jori to a different school. In the past, before going through my life-coaching training, a situation like this would have sent me into a temporary depression. I would feel the weight of it all and feel as though I couldn't get out from under it. I would feel sorry for myself or for Jori, or both of us sometimes, and think of how unfair it was that she had these struggles. These emotions would control me for days, until the impact had worn off a bit.

That's not what happened this time. Instead of immediately giving into the overwhelming emotions, I went to my bedroom, got on my knees and prayed. I told Heavenly Father every single thought and feeling I had. Then I got up, pulled out my patriarchal blessing and read it thoroughly, searching every line for a clue as to how to get through this. That's when I saw it,"...others will be given you to assist you..." Instead of drawing into myself and shutting the world out, I needed to reach out for help. Just as Elder Ross had been placed in my life to help me during my mission, I knew Heavenly Father had placed people in my life now to help me through this trial. I just had to figure out who they were. As Cameron and I talked about it later, he mentioned a friend of his who had a grown daughter with special needs that still lived with him and his wife. Cameron knew he would be happy to talk with us and give us advice as we embarked on this new, unknown territory.

We met this wonderful couple for dinner just a couple of nights later and that may be the best thing we could have done. While they listened and acknowledged the difficulties we were facing and would continue to face in the coming years, they were incredibly positive about the blessings that come with raising these special spirits. We left that night almost feeling as if we had won the lottery! And slowly, other pieces started to fit together that had perplexed me before. As difficult as Jori's behavior could be, I couldn't deny that people were drawn to her. Then the overpowering realization hit me: we weren't in her life to teach *her* in the normal sense; *she* was here to teach *us*. Jori has done what was required of her to return to live with her Heavenly Father. She is not on earth to learn the same things we are. Her purpose here is to teach. She teaches others about true, unconditional love, joy, and happiness just by being herself. She teaches me to be more patient (or at least try!) with others. She has bonded us with people we may have never known just because of their desire and the pull they feel to be in her life.

This was the biggest "trial" we have faced regarding Jori (up to this point) and it should have sent me spiraling into anger, sadness, and self-pity, based on my track record. But because Heavenly Father had guided me (through other people) into life-coaching, I was able to use what I had learned to reach out and find the people he had strategically placed in my life to assist me through this trial. I had the answers and support I needed to handle this. I just had to make the decision to look for them.

NINETEEN

Lesson Learned...FINALLY!

*I*t has taken several years and many uncanny experiences for this "control freak" to learn to release the control in my life. I look back and almost laugh at my feeble attempts to create the perfect life for myself. Sure, it might have been a fine life if everything had worked out as I wished. But it wouldn't be nearly as amazing and meaningful to me as it is now, having learned the lessons firsthand, that I needed to grow and become a better version of myself. The times of struggle and confusion have taught me patience and gratitude for what I had to work so hard for. The trials have humbled me and taught me empathy for others who may be experiencing a similar trial.

When I look at my life now, I see a wonderful, near-perfect husband (I mean that!) who came to me just the way I would have hoped. I see my two daughters who I had to struggle to have in my life, but who are direct blessings from a loving Heavenly Father. On those rough days as a mom, although I get frustrated, I don't take my role for granted. I remember the days when I would have given anything to be right where I am now. I am in a place I've always wanted to be: in a position to truly help others be happy with themselves and their loved ones. I have a stronger testimony of Heavenly Father and of Jesus Christ than I have ever had at any time in my life.

But I know that no matter what lies ahead for me, I have a Heavenly Father watching over me and guiding my steps and the steps of others to help me in my times of need. The lesson is to let Him have the control. He has the ability to make our lives better than we could ever have imagined. I am living proof of that.

I know that I will have trials in the future that will teach me a new lesson that I will need to know in order to continue to strengthen my testimony or to help another person, or hopefully both. But I know that no matter what lies ahead for me, I have a Heavenly Father watching over me and guiding my steps and the steps of others to help me in my times of need. The lesson is to let Him have the control. He has the ability to make our lives better than we could ever have imagined. I am living proof of that.

Acknowledgments

I am lucky to be surrounded by so many loving and influential people in my life. I would like to thank the following people for being a part of my journey and encouraging me to share it with the world.

To my parents—you both stood by me and supported me through every decision I made. Whether it was your ready advice or just your quiet presence, you seemed to always know just what I needed to grow. You both shared life lessons filled with wisdom that you probably thought I never really absorbed, but I still use many of those lessons in my life today. You somehow gave me the confidence to believe I could accomplish anything I could dream of, while still helping me see and accept reality in a healthy way when those dreams weren't meant to be. I am forever grateful to you, Mom, for teaching me to recognize God's voice so that when I couldn't reach you for help or advice, I could go to the one who knows all.

To my husband—you were a support to me long before you became my husband. Thank you for believing in every idea I come up with and for being the best "team player" and dad our girls could ask for. I couldn't have done this without you. Thank you for being my best friend. I love you more than you will ever know.

To my daughters, Haylee and Jori—you both were wanted and prayed for more than you will ever understand. You are my biggest blessings and I never take for granted the privilege it is to be your mom. Thank you for continuing to teach me how to be the best mom and person I can be. And thank you for your ready forgiveness when I mess it all up!

To my best friend, Kym Walsh—thank you for being by my side since the day we met July 24, 1994. You are the best cheerleader anyone could ask for. Thank you for reminding me of my potential when I can't see it. Thank you for encouraging me to get this book out to help other people. I am grateful every single day for your friendship.

To my first life coach ever, Cami DeWitt—thank you for following that prompting to reach out to me, even though you were nervous. Can you see now what you've ignited in my life? Without you, I would still be lost in life, wondering what my purpose was.

To Brenda Angle—thank you for creating The Faith-Based Life Coaching Academy. Thank you for using your own trials to create something so beautiful to bless the lives of countless coaches and people.

To my good friend, Heather McLeskey—thank you for giving so willingly of your time to proofread and edit my very rough draft of this book! I know Heavenly Father had a hand in bringing us together, not just for that purpose, but it is one I am incredibly grateful for.

To all my friends and family—thank you for having faith in me and my abilities. Thank you for cheering me on and encouraging me when I couldn't see what possibilities waited ahead of me.

To Melissa Jeanne—for being an answer to prayer without even realizing it. Thank you for making the changes in your life and writing your own book. You lit the path that led to me getting this book published. I am forever grateful to you.

To Jennifer Sparks at STOKE Publishing—thank you for all your work, ideas, and constant support in getting this book out to the world. You were the missing piece I had been searching for. I know I am not alone in thanking you for all you do for those of us with stories to tell.

Last, and most important, my thanks to my Heavenly Father, who has remained constant through my highs and lows. I know He has heard every prayer of gratitude, as well as every prayer whispered through tears of heartache and frustration. He continues to wait patiently as I learn the lessons I need to learn and blesses me every chance He can. My testimony of Him and of my Savior, Jesus Christ, gives my life meaning and purpose. It makes every trial worth it, and every victory that much sweeter.

About the Author

Bethany Comerford is a certified Faith-based Life Coach, speaker, and owner of Positive Connections Coaching. Through her coaching, she helps her clients take the steps necessary to truly find peace and joy in their lives, regardless of their circumstances. She also helps them create healthier relationships with the people in their lives. Bethany is also a certified Color Code Interpersonal Skills Workshop Facilitator. These workshops are presented to companies and groups to teach the participants how to read people more accurately, motivate others, and communicate more effectively.

Bethany is a mother to two daughters and wife to an avid Ironman triathlete. She enjoys spending time with friends, traveling, reading, and cheering on her husband at his races. Bethany lives in Gilbert, Arizona.

If you are interested in working with Bethany or having her speak at your event, you can email her at bcomerfordcoach@gmail.com or visit her website: www.positiveconnectionscoaching.com.

You can follow Bethany on social media at:

- Instagram: @positiveconnectionscoaching
- Facebook: Positive Connections Coaching.

Made in the USA
San Bernardino, CA
11 February 2020